AMERICA:

The

GREATEST

GOOD

by Nick A. Adams

www.nickadamsinamerica.com

iUniverse, Inc.

New York   Bloomington

America: The Greatest Good

iUniverse books may be ordered through booksellers or by contacting:

iUniverse
1663 Liberty Drive
Bloomington, IN 47403
www.iuniverse.com
1-800-Authors (1-800-288-4677)

Because of the dynamic nature of the Internet, any Web addresses or links contained in this book may have changed since publication and may no longer be valid. The views expressed in this work are solely those of the author and do not necessarily reflect the views of the publisher, and the publisher hereby disclaims any responsibility for them.

ISBN: 978-1-4502-5395-6 (sc)
ISBN: 978-1-4502-5396-3 (ebook)

Printed in the United States of America

iUniverse rev. date: 08/20/2010

The preservation of the sacred fire of liberty,
and the destiny of the republican model of government,
are justly considered as deeply, *perhaps as* finally, *staked on*
the experiment entrusted to the hands of the American people.

~George Washington, First Inaugural Address, 1789

TABLE OF CONTENTS

Foreword   i

Chapter 1
America: The Value-Driven Country   1

Chapter 2
Indivisible America   8

Chapter 3
Religion in America   18

Chapter 4
Our Troops   24

Chapter 5
A Culture of Exceptionalism   34

Chapter 6
Business and Consumerism   52

Chapter 7
Democracy and Politics   64

Chapter 8
Imperilled America   75

Chapter 9
How Greatness Endures: The Future   86

FOREWORD

ALMOST A HUNDRED AND EIGHTY YEARS AGO, a twenty-six-year-old Frenchman arrived on the shores of America to travel extensively across a young nation. Five years later, he wrote about the greatness of America. His name was Alexis de Tocqueville. This year, 2010, marks the one hundred and seventy fifth birthday of his prophetic masterpiece, entitled *Democracy in America*. During the almost two centuries since, there has been a conspicuous dearth of recorded foreign observation and analysis of the greatness of America.

Tocqueville's book remains the only time in the history of America that a foreigner, an outsider, has written a comprehensive account of his journey through America, focusing solely on American exceptionalism.

The world was a starkly different place when Tocqueville penned his masterwork—framed around his travels with his friend to America—now considered a classic of sociology and political science. While some elements are outdated, the book's substantive content is as accurate and piercingly relevant as it was nearly two centuries ago.

I believe a new book on American greatness from an external source is well overdue, and that such a work could not come at a more poignant time, when some critics are

i

predicting the slow decrepitude of America and the rise of China. Even more, I consider it essential that, once again, an outside voice express the potential that this country has to offer human civilisation.

In this vein, I am disappointed that it has taken so long for a non-American to write about America's greatness, given the tremendous debt of gratitude the world owes to America for her continual pursuit and protection of freedom and democracy around the globe.

In 2009, as a twenty-four-year-old Australian, I arrived on the shores of America to travel extensively across the country. I crisscrossed the nation from West Coast to East Coast, from North to South, visiting nineteen states. The purpose of my visit was to observe, and also to speak to many different associations, policy institutes, community groups, and grassroots citizen organisations. The theme of my speeches was: why I believe America epitomises greatness.

I have felt impelled to write this book for some time, as I have been appalled by the constant, ever-increasing, inane, and fatuous anti-Americanism across the world, but had I done so without visiting the country, my views would have been vulnerable to attack by detractors. America—her people and her culture—was everything I expected and much more.

I travelled through the nation by plane, train, car, bus, and horse and cart. I saw small town America and big city America. I stayed in hotels, farms, apartments, houses, villas, and mansions. I visited rolling hills, deserts, bright city lights, forests, factories, parks, museums, and rodeos. I experienced history, culture, recreation and industry, the past and present, the fun and the work. I saw firsthand examples of American brilliance in entrepreneurial innovation. I met with Mayors, Congressmen, businessmen, and critical analysis as framed through the experiences of my life, my upbringing as an Australian, my personal ideology, and my extensive travels across the world, including being schooled partly in Germany. Some Americans may say that my analyses of components of American culture are naïve and that I am hideously optimistic. I say to those people that I have fresh and unique eyes, and accept the advantages and disadvantages that these bring. All I can do, as did Thucydides twenty-four hundred years ago, is offer my work, not as a politically captivating tabloid designed for instant gratification but, rather, as a personal testament intended for future generations.

In the same way, the forecasts I offer about the greatness of America in this century and beyond are not supported by empirical data or an army of footnotes. Rather, I draw on my education, cultural analysis, 'gut feeling', and confidence as an individual to make educated calculations. If you would dismiss this approach, do not read the book.

I believe I have something priceless to offer both the American populace and the world in writing this book. Many have called my endeavour 'the Tocqueville of this generation'. I am flattered by this description and feel that if I can make even a fraction of the contribution to American pride and culture that de Tocqueville did, I will be deeply gratified.

In the acknowledgments at the end of the book, I attempt to appropriately express my gratitude— though no "thank you" could be fully adequate—to all of those who had so much to do with its creation and completion. There is, however, an exception.

I want to thank, first and foremost, America—her military and her people. I wish to thank them for their leadership of the world and their undying friendship of freedom and democracy. I and generations of others all around the world have been tremendously happy and inspired to live in a world led by you. Thank you for preserving the principles that lie in the bedrock of your country: freedom, liberty, justice, democracy, and bravery. Thank you for spreading those principles and protecting freedom at an enormous cost. I appreciate you and applaud you.

God Bless You, God Bless America, and may she long reign over this earth.

Nick Adams
Moree, Australia
July 2010

AMERICA: THE VALUE-DRIVEN COUNTRY

America is great because she is good.
If America ceases to be good, America will cease to be great.

~Alexis de Tocqueville, *Democracy in America*

TO UNDERSTAND AMERICA'S GREATNESS, one must understand her values: those social constants which determine, transform, and ultimately transcend their society. The values-oriented culture that has existed from the time of foundation has defined America's experience and delivered American exceptionalism in the form of the greatest and most powerful country in the world's history. The United States of America is the only values-driven country in the world today. The last half-century has seen the nations of Europe grappling with identity, political correctness, and permissiveness, while in the former USSR and China, the decrepit ideological edifice of Marxism-Leninism has fallen, only to be replaced by a toxic cocktail of blended authoritarianism and racism masquerading as nationalism, without any international appeal. Only America's values set has been robust and unyielding, and has only increased in utility. The dilution, erosion, and ignorance of values across the world due to a lack of courage to pursue them has seen nations become subject to inherent internal instability, self-doubt, and ambiguity.

This begs the question: Why the stark contrast? The answer can be found in the enduring principles of America's founding. The fact is that American values are far superior to those of any other nation in their combination of strength and unity, with limitless individualism. The measure of enduring greatness of a nation is her founding principles. If great principles lie at the core of a nation, the nation is destined to be great. The principles that lie at the bedrock of the United States of America are political freedom, personal liberty, justice, democracy, and bravery. An American lives in the most prosperous land in the history of the world. The root of that prosperity can be found in the Declaration of Independence, which recognises the God-given right of each person to the pursuit of happiness. The US Constitution also entrenches core, inalienable, democratic rights.

All of this is intimately interconnected and intricately interwoven. An unbreakable spine allows for inspiration to thrive and to prosper. America sells inspiration like no other nation. Whereas other countries deride dreams and dreamers, Americans seek constantly to live a dream—to pursue happiness, as their Constitution provides.

Values underpin every area of strength in America. Whether it is the pre-eminence of religion, intense and muscular patriotism, enviable unity, or omnipresence of the military in their culture, every aspect is derived from the values-centric society that it is. Values are the link and explanation of why everything is the way it is in America.

From enduring principles, come enduring values. The greatest evidence of the strength of American values, aside from longevity, is their transcending of political agendas. While there may be disagreement on the interpretation of these values, political activists of both the left and right acknowledge the existence of these values. Through Democratic and Republican administrations, natural and industrial disasters, financial crises and international conflicts, America endures because it has an unbreakable backbone.

It is one thing to have enduring principles and values; it is another matter entirely to celebrate those principles and values continuously and uniformly. The majority of Western countries endow their citizens with liberties and freedoms similar to America's, yet none celebrate their existence with anywhere near the same intensity. Take for example, the ultimate value of freedom in the rest of the world, even the Western world. Western countries enjoy and support the same core freedoms, but cultural references in their respective societies are conspicuously absent, as are public references to it by government officials or political leaders. Other countries are afraid to speak of their values, or possess none. No other population outside of America genuinely asserts that their belief in such values affords them a moral superiority.

In addition, a diluted and thus directionless culture, where values are barely referenced, presents enormous problems for the potential integration of new immigrants. In other Western democracies, recent immigrants can at best make vague references to a 'better life', yet many in these countries insist on preserving their place of origin to the point where it competes with and, at worst usurps, the culture of their current country. There is a later chapter in this book that discusses the 'melting pot' of America in greater detail. Suffice it to say that as I travelled through America, and canvassed immigrants, both old and recently arrived, each acknowledged and articulated that it was the values system of America and the focus on opportunity that brought them to America. Again, it is America's nature as a values-driven society that allows for it to bear the mantle of 'the land of opportunity'.

The 'American contract' is the greatest contract in the history of world civilisation. Some nations find their unity to be automatic. Some are deeply rooted in birth. Others are deeply rooted in blood. America does not have any of those luxuries. Instead, she relies on the unity of a transcendental set of values that formulate citizenship. Here, as elsewhere, the Civil War of the nineteenth century provides the exception that proves the rule where two competing ideas of liberty collided and ultimately fused. The 'American contract' is both disinterested and uninterested in an applicant's background and beliefs. Provided the applicant is prepared to exhibit loyalty to the set of ideals that is America, the American people and their contract welcome you. A stronger bond than the 'American contract' cannot be found on the planet. It is a national identity that is based solely on values. The founders of America were highly suspicious of democracy and never considered it, favouring a Republic. It was to be a government of laws, not men. The same applies to the 'American contract'.

The emphasis on values allows Americans to be confident and to encourage a culture of putting America first, while simultaneously welcoming those with new perspectives and new influences. This is the primary reason that America, unlike its Western counterparts and cousins, does not encounter tremendous difficulty with its Muslim populations. Muslims in America, by and large, put America first. By and large, American Muslims tend to be far less radical and, for those of that faith, America comes before Islam. The noxious weed of home-grown terrorism cannot flourish. (Rare instances are the April 1995 bombing of the Murrah Federal Building in Oklahoma City and the Fort Hood massacre in November 2009.) This set of circumstances can be achieved only in a strong culture where values are a way of life and underpin patriotism and unity. Consider the strength of a country in which, through one common set of values, opposite sides of the political spectrum unite to reach the same conclusion. There is no better example than the overarching view of Muslim populations worldwide. The political Right's detestation of Muslims is derived from the Islamic faith, and the Left's detestation is derived from the inherently conservative nature of Islamic culture and their treatment of women.

Perhaps the greatest example of the value-centric society of America can be found in the application of the value of freedom. There is no uncertainty: Americans are the embodiment of the spirit of human freedom. Americans rejoice every day that they are free. "Thank God we are free!" is the catchcry from all Americans. Through the example of freedom, one can also observe that it is not a value or principle subject to political persuasion; in fact, past Presidents and Presidential candidates of all stripes, left and right, have praised and acknowledged the pursuit of freedom.

Americans are incapable of taking for granted freedom and democracy through the huge presence of the military in their culture. They are all touched by the enormous price that their nation has paid to spread these ideals around the world. Freedom will be defended no matter what. Young American men love and believe in freedom so much that they travel around the world, sustaining horrific injuries, losing limbs, eyesight, and even life itself so that someone they do not even know, someone they have never met, can have freedom. The inspiration of America is breathtaking.

America is a young nation, still shy of the maturity indicative of adulthood. As such, there is a dimension of rawness to it that presents it with even greater capacity to allow for values to become self-evident truths and, in turn, for America to thrive and prosper. Consider the biggest and strongest seventeen-year-old, who happens to be the star quarterback and student at the local school, and who comes from a family of committed Christians. He holds his values as patently true and is more inclined to fight for them than is a mature adult. Anyone who believes that America is diminishing in world superpower status is gravely mistaken. Through the culture of America, we see that America is just at the beginning of its powers. The overwhelming power of its values and its founding principles (its uniqueness in being intentionally brought into being) also suggest that it is less likely that it will ever succumb to external cultural influences and disintegrate into decadence as has happened to the entire European continent and all former world superpowers from the Romans to the Byzantines, Abassids, Ottomans, and Khans.

The values-emphasis of America is the envy of the world. Such jealously is the root of all anti-Americanism and the source of the extreme hatred many harbour. It is also the simplest explanation of why the evil events of September 11th transpired. Here's a question: How is it that the country with just five percent of the world's population creates the majority of the world's wealth? Or controls the world's sea, air, and space and is the most powerful superpower in world history? Common sense dictates that it must be doing something right. What makes it so great that people feel the need to cowardly hijack planes and slam them into buildings? It is the strength of their values system. Make no mistake, both the Afghanistan and Iraq conflicts are culture wars—further evidence of the values-driven culture of the United States.

To continue to lead the world, all the United States needs to do is stay true to its values as its age increases and not fall into the negative trappings of what many self-anointed 'statesmen' call 'maturity', not seek to compromise with ideologies antithetical to its very existence or succumb to the myopia of relativism—the moral equivalent of dope. Just as the then twenty-seven-year-old de Tocqueville predicted some two hundred years ago the age of American pre-eminence, I forecast ongoing and increasing American dominance throughout the twenty-first century and beyond.

INDIVISIBLE AMERICA

*I pledge allegiance to the Flag of the United States of America,
and to the Republic for which it stands, one Nation under God,
indivisible, with liberty and justice for all.*

The Pledge of Allegiance to the United States Flag

A STRING OF THIRTY-ONE WORDS, recited by citizens standing and facing the American flag, with their right hands over their hearts, imbues a people with an unshakeable unity and patriotism.

The Pledge of Allegiance to the United States flag is possibly the best example of American patriotism and explanation of America's strength. There is not an American unable to recite the words of the Pledge, by heart. School children recite the Pledge daily. Public meetings and events are begun with the Pledge. Congressional sessions begin with the recitation.

It was an incredible experience to stand amid Americans at the beginning of public events and meetings and to witness firsthand the swift, automatic shuffle of feet and turning of bodies toward wherever the American flag was hanging. For a form of words recited so often, I expected those present to simply recite the words automatically, free of emotion. It was with great surprise and delight that the voices I heard rang with passion; and as I looked around to observe the faces of the people, I saw fixed eyes, stern concentration, and earnestness commensurate with the gravity of the words. From a cacophony of voices came a united chorus.

I cannot think of another country in the world that has an equivalent of this Pledge to the values of liberty and justice, and its frequent recitation.

My first taste of American patriotism occurred on Australian soil in 2006 when I had the pleasure of meeting a bright, then-twenty-four-year-old American university exchange student from Florida who had just completed her pre-med studies at Harvard. She came from a very distinguished family with proud traditions. She and her family were all registered Democrats, and one of her older brothers was a high-powered lawyer—so high-powered in fact, that he was one of the personal legal assistants for the Democratic Presidential candidate John Kerry during the 2004 US election. She made it clear in no uncertain terms that she disliked George W. Bush, both on a personal level and in his capacity as US President. Then she said, "But he's my president and I respect his office and I am behind him one hundred percent." While not disagreeing with her sentiments, but wanting to labour the point, I asked her if she felt that that compromised her principles. Her reply came with the speed of reflex: "No, I may not like Bush, but he's the president of what I believe is the greatest country in the world, my country, and he deserves my support."

I remember thinking: "Wow! What a country!" With citizens like these, it is not difficult to see how the United States rose to superpower status and why it continues to be the strongest and greatest nation in the world.

Again, in early January 2007, on Australian soil, I was reminded of American patriotism when I heard an awe-inspiring story over dinner. The lady who told the story was a primary school teacher who taught in a suburban Sydney school. She recounted the arrival of two US children at her school, one aged six and another slightly younger. Brother and sister, both were the children of parents whose occupation required them to relocate continually. The parents informed the school that both children had been diagnosed with dyslexia and that they had been struggling academically. My friend had been given the duty of assessing the children in order to place them appropriately within the curriculum. She discovered that their academic performance was, indeed, very poor, and they struggled with even the most basic of tasks, such as writing their names. Right at the end of the assessment, she asked each if there was an achievement from their old school that they would like to share with her — to show her something that they could do. "We can name every state in America, and every President of United States of America, in order," the children responded. My friend then watched in complete amazement as each child rattled off the name of every state and every President in the history of the United States, beginning with George Washington, and ending with George W. Bush. In her words: "Here were children who could not write their names on a piece of a paper but had committed to memory so much about their country. What an education system they must have over there."

To understand America's greatness, one must understand her patriotism. While some Americans declare concern that the strength of patriotism has deteriorated from what it used to be, and that political correctness is diluting patriotism, they do not realise how strong American patriotism is, compared with that of other nations. I see such a view as emblematic of a wider inclination to nostalgia. By the same token, the few Americans who believe that patriotism is overdone and unnecessary in their country do not realise their patriotism is one of the keys to American strength, unity, inclusion, and dominance.

As an outsider looking in, with objective and general eyes, I can see the fervour of American patriotism and its brilliance. I can compare it to that of my own nation— another great, free, democratic, successful Western country, but without the pride, patriotism, or unity.

The most impressive aspect of American culture and the American people is patriotism. The most common sight in America is an American flag. Surely the visibility of a country's flag within its own borders is a measure of its greatness and strength. Wherever one travels, whether in small town America or big city America, regardless of population or demographics, clean and crisp flags adorn streets, shopping centres, buildings, homes, graves, letterboxes, taxis, buses, and petrol stations. Walking and driving through streets, with flags everywhere, I felt a strange sense of reassurance, of comfort, of inclusion. This begged the question: If I can feel this way as a visitor, as a tourist, then what effect must this have on the American psyche?

One illustration of this was shared with me by a friend who, while studying in China, roomed with a Californian student at their university dorm. This young man approached my friend, expressing a desire to hang up his American flag on the outside of their door. The approach was polite but firm and confident, and my friend felt unable to express any opposition to a suggestion put so reasonably. My friend was amazed at the intense pride in his country that had inspired his roommate to carry his flag half way around the world and his eagerness to proclaim it in a foreign country. No one else does that.

Foreign critics of America, particularly many of the Western intelligentsia, attack American patriotism, labelling it with adjectives such as 'jingoistic', 'nationalistic, or 'brainwashing', and calling it 'embarrassing'. They even try to portray 'the hand over the heart' and the 'facial expression' as something to send up as humourous.

There is nothing embarrassing or comical about American patriotism or nationalism. The roots of all the criticisms levelled at America stem from the most corrosive element of human nature: jealousy. In fact, American patriotism is the envy of the world. In countries harbouring such sentiments, the Right base their dislike on envy that their nations are unable to reach such patriotic heights, and the Left dislike it because it is American.

Such criticisms also fail to take into account fundamental differences in culture and personality between America and other nations: the fact that Americans, unlike most cultures, are a completely unreserved and very passionate and emotional people. This lack of reservedness and presence of emotion is manifested in the acts associated with patriotism.

Patriotism and nationalism are virtues of a country that should be hotly pursued. Patriotism unites a people: it provides the glue to a society. There is nothing intrinsically wrong with loving one's country. There is no aspect more fundamental to the success of a nation; patriotism has a pervasive effect on every facet of human nature. It is responsible for the confidence and assuredness of a people and for the incentive to be exceptional. Its impact on education is extraordinary. It affects a people from birth to death. The American citizen is entirely unselfish in remembering the country in which he or she lives and regards every achievement of America as a personal victory. Patriotism, when it is based on transcendent values like liberty, justice, and democracy — as it is in America — is particularly potent.

As I travelled through the country, I was struck by the boundless patriotism, flag-waving, and pro-American language used by leaders on both sides of politics. This impressed me deeply as it was in stark contrast to the rest of the Western world today, where anyone who dares mention patriotism and displays pride in his or her national identity is instantly accused of jingoism and xenophobia, and must be a simplistic, uneducated, slack-jawed, redneck. Not so in the United States, where patriotism is loud and proud — the way it should be.

Take the example of the singing of the national anthem at public events. As a very proud Australian, it hurts me to say that I find it embarrassing to see the lack of enthusiasm and passion when the Australian anthem is sung at our public events. Such an observation is not exclusive to Australia; in fact it can be seen throughout Western nations around the world. It is in stark contrast to the American national anthem experience, which sees the anthem sung with intensity and concentration, and with the hand placed over the heart. Such an example may appear trivial, but it exemplifies a self-destructive quality within the Australian national character that still seems to be prevalent among the majority. This trait simply does not exist in the American national character, and the country is better for it.

The United States is the most successful country in the world through its melting pot. The concept of the 'melting pot', virtually synonymous with the United States, is the ultimate manifestation of American power and patriotism. Countries worldwide struggle with their immigrant populations, yet the United States has flourished because of them. American citizens' loyalty to the United States never appears in doubt, ethnic heritage notwithstanding—a situation other Western countries covet. The common concerns today in countries such as Germany, Britain, France and Australia are that many of their immigrant arrivals feel a greater loyalty to their countries of birth or heritage. With respect to the 'multiculturalism' policies of every country in the Western world, it needs to be said: You cannot believe in everything, because if you believe in everything, then you believe in nothing.

America has never had and never will have these problems which engender weakness because it believes in something. This is again all a product of the values-centric society that is America, and those values come first. Such values lead to the pursuit of cultural assimilation and acculturation. The key distinction between America and other countries is that America's emphasis is the unity of shared values. It is about being one. This concept is even imbedded in the great seal of the United States: *E Pluribus Unum*—Out of Many, One.

Studying the scripted language of politicians is often a useful exercise in analysing culture. The words chosen reflect not just what the particular audience wishes to hear, but also the path that politician deems the most conducive to securing votes. As such, it is fascinating that in America the cultural spotlight on unity is echoed in the speech and communication of political leaders. By contrast, most Western democratic governments seldom refer to unity and adhere to a strategy of divide and conquer, as the implementation of this strategy has been shown to be the best way of winning elections. Yet again, the value of unity is one emphasised by both the Right and Left in America.

Critics of America conveniently ignore the success and ambition of the American project and its enormous contribution to civilisation. Where recent history has shown us that the rest of the world seeks the division of nations into micro-states to resolve matters of conflict, America hosts an incredibly large and diverse population, living under the one federal government, in peace.

If patriotism is a key to America's strength, then what is the key to the strength and effectiveness of patriotism? The answer is simple. It is repetition. Repetition is the motherhood of retention. Patriotic repetition in America is not just limited to the recital of the Pledge of Allegiance, or the omnipresence of the flag. It travels far deeper, and the great trait of patriotism is that it permeates through to the basics of life and business and becomes a way of life. Repetition and metastasis are continuous cycles, feeding from each other. The use of the red, white, and blue colours is everywhere; businesses use them for their logos, sporting teams use them for their mascots, store owners paint their shop facades in these colours. Casinos have slot machines whose exteriors are laden with patriotic American symbols and emblems. There is a chain of petrol stations called 'Freedom'. In America, even Coca-Cola cans have stars and stripes.

Another highly visible example of instilling pride is that all across America the names of streets, the names of cities, the names of restaurants, the names of businesses and casinos often have some American cultural or historical connection. I found street names possibly the greatest example. I came across Liberty Avenues, Independence Avenues, Philadelphia Streets, Washington Drives, and Freedom Lanes all across America, even in residential areas close to small towns. In Nashville, I saw Rosa L. Parks Avenue. Atlanta and many other cities across America boast a Martin Luther King Drive. Las Vegas has a Dean Martin Drive. Memphis is home to Elvis Presley Boulevard.

In Washington, DC, many streets bear the names of early states in the Union—as well as patriotic terms like Independence and Constitution—the most famous being Pennsylvania Avenue, on which the White House stands. Many other American cities also have streets named after states and famous places. I noticed a Hollywood Casino in central Pennsylvania. I stayed at Hotel Pennsylvania when in New York. Many buildings in Washington DC are named after Presidents or other prominent former statesmen.

What effect does all this have? It is an example of pervasive patriotism where one is constantly reminded of the history of one's country, the famous people who have shaped it, and the big cities that are famous. It presents the feeling of living in a bubble—that all that you need, the heart and centre of the world, is in America. If you recite a meaningful pledge every day and live in a country where the American flag is visually embedded in daily life, where patriotic banners hang off the awnings of homes, a love for one's country becomes a part of the subconscious. That is how you build and maintain a great country. Patriotism fits well into the American ethos, one that can be described as a 'crusading ethos'—confident, without the shadow of doubt, forceful, fearless, aggressive, and always with a presence that is impossible to describe. Just spend half an hour at the National Museum of Patriotism in Atlanta and you will know what I mean.

If ever you wanted measurement of the indivisibility and sense of identity, as well as emotional intelligence of Americans, I offer this experience. I had the great fortune of spending Thanksgiving 2009 in the Carolinas with a wonderful American family. They lived in Lexington, a suburb of Columbia, South Carolina. As one of the days was drawing to a close, and having toured the sites of significance already, the eldest son thought that he might as well show me Lexington's main strip, it having little tourist quality. As we were driving through a fairly normal and nondescript area, with few businesses and nary a hint of activity near the local municipal buildings, I was stunned to see a huge monument on the side of the road that resembled three firefighters looking at the remains of one of the World Trade Center towers. I enquired about it and asked to stop. It was indeed a 9/11 Memorial monument or sculpture that had been commissioned by the Leadership Lexington Class of 2007 in time to be unveiled for the seventh anniversary of the attacks of September 2001. As I studied it carefully, and read its plaques, its size was not its only surprise; the level of detail in the sculpture to represent Shanksville, Pennsylvania, the Pentagon, and the World Trade Center was breathtaking. All this was in a town or suburb of about fourteen thousand people, a long way from the green pastures of Pennsylvania, the politics of Washington, or the chaos of New York City sidewalks. It made me wonder just how many Lexington, South Carolinas there are out there all across the nation; and it made me realise how great American unity, remembrance, and patriotism are. The truth is that America is full of Lexingtons, filled with the same heart, spirit, and indivisibility.

RELIGION IN AMERICA

*The Americans combine the notions of religion and liberty
so intimately in their minds, that it is impossible
to make them conceive of one without the other.*

~Alexis de Tocqueville, *Democracy in America*

IT IS NOT UNTIL YOU VISIT THE CHURCHES of America, that you recognise America's greatness.

I identify myself as a Christian and use Christianity as a moral compass, but I do not consider myself especially religious, nor do I regularly attend church. There is no conscious reason for this, and perhaps it is more the product of the culture of the country I live in than of personal predilection.

Religion underpins American society and culture and provides her with self-belief, morality, clarity of thought, strength of spirit, and courage of conviction. You cannot escape God as you travel through America; even to the agnostic, He lifts you, He reassures you, and He guides you and your country.

"God Bless America" is a frequent refrain. It can be found on bumper stickers, on billboards on the side of roads, in the speeches of politicians, and in the lyrics of songs. Much like patriotic fervour, God is everywhere.

Inscribed on every coin and written on every currency note are the words "In God We Trust".

I found in my travels that this robustness of religion does vary from state to state. Anyone who believes, however, that such fervent religiosity exists only in the so-called 'Bible Belt' of the Deep South is sorely mistaken. Christianity is an integral element in even the most progressive of communities in the major cities of both the East and West coasts.

There may be some Americans who express concern and dare I say it, embarrassment, at the religious fervour exhibited by many of their fellow Americans; but if they were to look at the general effect of religion on their country throughout their history, I believe they would recognise that the concept far outweighs their general and, to my mind, unwarranted concerns. It is often forgotten that the most murderous regimes of the last century—Nazi Germany and the Soviet Union—were both avowedly atheistic.

Christianity is permanently etched into the American psyche, and this is reflected in the belief that all Americans passionately hold: that they are "one Nation under God". Religiosity in America is permanent and pervasive, while political correctness and the intellectual elite tear down religion around the world. As a result, religion in other Western countries is characterised by lethargy, dwindling church attendance, an emphasis on secularity, and an almost total dearth of the concept of individual charity— which is the most prominent manifestation of religion in America.

The most refreshing aspect of Americans and their religion is their openness in expressing their deep and abiding faith, a severe contrast to the reserved and private religiosity of people of other free, democratic Western countries.

One of the most memorable experiences in my life came when I attended a general Sunday Service at the First Assembly of God Church in Normal, Illinois. Until then, my experiences in churches of the Anglican, Catholic, and Orthodox Christian denominations had led me to associate church services with silence, formality, and restraint. As soon as I entered the doors of this church, I was astonished as I heard enthusiastic, boisterous voices singing.

When I first laid eyes on the congregation, I was floored. I saw a congregation swaying almost in unison, with arms and palms outstretched upwards, and an incessant tapping of feet. Even the elderly and disabled seated, unable to rise, rocked forward and backward, almost as if in trance. The music was not of the traditional hymn variety; its music was uplifting, energetic, and catchy, with simple, repetitive lyrics. Everything from even the physical setup of the church lent itself to informality and collective prayer. Built in a semicircle, surrounding a stage where a band composed of all types of congregation members (young, old, male, female, black, white), it had more the feel of being in a school hall, learning the music and dancing of an upcoming school dance. Throughout the service, the congregation sang, danced, and moved as if declaring their love for life and existence. Throughout the sermon of the pastor, members of the congregation would nod vigorously in approval, spontaneously declaring aloud "That's right!", "Hallelujah!", "Yes!", "Amen!", "Thank you, Lord!", and "Bless me!"

What are the benefits of such religiosity? The first point to make is that irrespective of your own personal religious faith, you cannot deny the positive, calming, humanitarian and philanthropic influence that Christianity has had in the building of the American nation. Nor is it conceivable to suggest that even a benign belief in God is in any way of negative impact to an individual or a community. In fact, religion, much like patriotism, has a pervasively positive influence—on morale, confidence and unity. When culture is as immersed in religion as it is in America, it is reflected in the everyday confidence and assuredness of its citizens. It is belief in God that makes America strong and contributes to her confidence.

Many non-Americans often marvel at how articulate Americans of all stripes are. It is almost impossible to find an American unable to express themselves well. While some of this must be apportioned to the strength of the American education system and patriotism, I believe that much of it also has to do with the presence of religion and the attendance at church services. This should occasion no surprise as the modern English tongue was born in the minds of Wycliffe and Tyndale as they set about translating the inaccessible Latin scriptures into the common speech of England. The greatest and most inspirational public speaking comes from America, much of it derived from religious leaders. In just two hours at a service, I was awash with heightened language. If you imagine, all across America, young aspiring Americans listening to ministers and pastors who preach with educated zeal and verbal artistry, shaping words to sharpen minds, reviving spirits, relieving the vulnerable and uplifting the downcast, it is not difficult to fathom why Americans impress with their presentation and elegance of expression. Eloquence comes with self-belief and confidence, and religion provides that confidence in the American culture. The resulting benefits for industry and the private sector from such articulation and presentation requires no further labour.

In a later chapter, I will discuss one cornerstone of American greatness in culture—the practice of consumerism. Suffice it to say that, as with everything else, religion, unlike in most parts of the world, is consumed in America. The American people are an emotional lot, and religion, simply put, makes people emotional and makes them believe. Here, again, is an example of how the inherently unreserved, emotional, and passionate nature of Americans allows them to capitalise on the positive aspects of worship and gives them the strength to lead the world.

The experience of attending church in America made me want to return—left me hungry for more, despite not being a regular churchgoer. It was free of stuffiness. Everything seemed much more accessible. Of course, not all churches in America provide the same relaxed climate, but with a church like this, it is not too difficult to see why the strength of religion in America has withstood the passage of time.

The simple reality is that only in America would such a church survive. A friend of mine in Australia attended a one-off Christian outreach event run by the Hillsong Church in Australia. According to my friend, this pastor was one of the most inspiring and engaging speakers he had ever heard. As he built his sermon to a crescendo, in front of the ten-thousand-strong crowd, he then yelled out: "If you want to be saved, stand up right now! Stand up to be saved! Stand up now!" In a crowd of ten thousand, only three people stood up. This prompted the pastor to say "Wow, are you guys a tough crowd or what? I mean I knew the British were reserved, but you guys take the cake!" While most of those ten thousand people were strongly religious, they refused to stand out from the crowd and publicly express their faith. This is where American culture differs.

I was interested to discover that unlike most of Europe and the Western world, the US government forbids direct funding of religious organisations, the greatest indication of secularity. This means that houses of worship must compete for membership and private support, as they cannot rely on the resources of the government when times are tough. So what happens? Much like capitalism under the invisible hand, religion flourishes. It is a great irony that those countries whose governments fund religious organisations directly pride themselves on their secularity.

Unlike in most other nations, the freedom to practise any religion is enshrined by the Constitution in America. This is another stark difference from many other countries and continents that have sought to ensure the church plays no role in state affairs. The unassailable fact is that many of the virtues and values of America have come from religious guidance, and it is a better nation for it. A belief in Providence, at the core of the founding in America and in the average American life, is truly America's greatest weapon and its greatest distinction from any other nation in the world.

The religiosity of Americans is enduring. Some one hundred and seventy-five years ago, Tocqueville noted, when visiting churches, that America was great because of God and religion. This is as true today as it was then. America's strength derives from its religiosity, and Americans' willingness to publicly express their faith provides them with the firmest of footholds to lead the world with conviction and courage, as they have. Americans must never forget that virtue cannot be sustained if religion is absent; and if virtue is absent, then liberty, too, must be absent. This simple equation, and the fact that America gets it right, speak volumes about the reasons for the greatness and success of America.

OUR TROOPS

War is an ugly thing, but not the ugliest of things.
The decayed and degraded state of moral and patriotic feeling
that thinks nothing worth a war is worse.

~John Stuart Mill, British philosopher

AT THE CORE OF ANY GREAT NATION is a strong military, but a strong military does not automatically make a great nation.

America is, without doubt, home to the finest military in the world. Some even suggest the finest the world has ever seen. Achieving this mantle is not necessarily just the product of spending and training, the same way that having a strong military does not instantly qualify a nation as a great one. Instead, it is the way that a country's culture and people incorporate the military into their everyday lives that demonstrates greatness.

One of the most forceful influences on American culture is its military and military history. America adores and respects its military. It gets emotional about its military history. Military service in America is considered the greatest service to country. Every American family seems to have been touched at some time or another by the military.

Travelling through America on my speaking tour, if I ever paused for a moment to reflect on and thank the American men and women currently serving abroad and protecting world interests, it would be common to see eyes moisten with silent weeping.

If someone asked me to pinpoint the time when I became overwhelmed by America's greatness, and when I first recognised its unparalleled strength, I'd say it was an experience at Atlanta airport. I was sitting at my gate, red-eyed, getting ready to board my plane, when suddenly I was awakened from my slumber by people all around me shouting and gesturing excitedly. Within twenty seconds, every person at my gate had stood, and deafening applause had begun. I, too, stood, wondering what had happened. To my amazement, as I looked around, as far as the eye could see, every single person in that section of the airport had stopped cold, and was now smiling, applauding, and cheering. Even airport staff, even people lined up for coffee at a nearby coffee shop — everyone was applauding wildly. Then I saw it: forty or so troops, dressed in full military attire, with travel bags over their shoulders, returning home for the July Fourth weekend. This experience numbed me with pride, and goose bumps covered my arms.

Australia, by contrasting illustration, in spite of its small population, has a tremendous military. The Australian SASR troops — Special Air Service Regiment, in charge of reconnaissance and counter-terrorism missions — are said to be the best and most highly skilled in the world. Throughout my travels, whenever meeting men who have served with Australians, be it in Vietnam, Korea, Afghanistan, or Iraq — they were, without exception, glowing in their praise of the Australians with whom they had served. Each commented specifically on the honour and bravery of the Australian men and women alongside whom they had served. Unfortunately, in Australia, public sentiment toward our military is not at the same level of appreciation. Similarly unappreciative attitudes exist in virtually all other Western democracies — except for the United States, which again leads the world.

In any conversation about the military, the issue of war must be addressed. Foreign detractors of America invariably suggest that America is a nation replete with warmongers and bereft of morality in such pursuits. The suggestion that America is morally impoverished, given that it is often at war, is preposterous. To the contrary, it is because America is a values-driven country where morality reigns supreme that it is so often at war. It has transformed necessary wars of self-defence in Afghanistan and Iraq into campaigns to spread positive values. The United States has not gone to wars for territory, or treasure or oil as was charged in the Iraq war. It expends its effort in spreading its virtues to the corners of the world. I believe American action to liberate societies, eliminate threats, and set societies on course for a new and improved direction is entirely legal and fair. It is categorical: the United States has never in its entire history entered a war without a genuine moral reason.

Since the beginning of the twentieth century, the United States has been at war almost continuously. While it has come at great cost, war has been the great purgative for America. War is the evil necessity for its economic and security strategy. Facts must be faced: It has been America's military spending that has often rescued its economy from periods of sluggishness. The late ending of the Great Depression is often attributed to America's delayed involvement in the Second World War. As for security strategy: So long as there is instability in other parts of the world, America's security prospers, as the evil forces are unable to unite and concentrate their efforts on America. Unlike other nations across the world in history who have lost time because of their involvement in war, America, when it has waged war, has continued to flourish. Continual American participation in wars has increased patriotism, fortified morale, and bolstered unity.

The United States controls the air, the seas, and outer space. It has naval bases around the world, allowing it to control both the Pacific and Atlantic Oceans. Although not unprecedented, it is the first world superpower in history to have accomplished this on such a scale that the rest of the world's navies put together are still no match for America's. Such control is not accidental; in fact, it exhibits another example of American military tactical brilliance, strategic direction, and forward planning. A note of interest: China, widely considered likely to become the next world superpower did not, until recently, even have a navy—a fact not known by many, and one that reinforces the enormous chasm between America and the rest of the world in military might. In spite of this supreme power and capability, America generally has been exceptionally moderate in its use of force.

There are certain distinct natural advantages to the United States in terms of its security. Geographically, America is blessed. With Canada to its north and Mexico to its South, the United States is afforded the luxury of being confident in the knowledge that they will not be attacked by neighbouring countries. Almost uniquely, America has not fought a war with one of its neighbours for more than a century.

If you ever wanted evidence of the influence and significance of the military in the United States, look no further than 'the Crossroads of the World'—Times Square, in New York City. Directly in the centre of Times Square is an Armed Forces Recruiting Station. Could you imagine this in London or Berlin or Tokyo or Sydney? The experience of walking into Times Square for the first time and observing that military recruitment station is one that will hold a permanent place in my mind. It is not possible to find a more suitable embodiment of American greatness and superiority.

I had the great honour of meeting currently serving members of the US military throughout my trip across America. Whether it was in a highway truck stop just outside of Canton, Mississippi, or on the streets in Washington DC, I was struck by their decorum and affability. Seeing everyday people stop in the streets to wave, salute, say thank you, or just give the 'thumbs-up' sign was heartening.

On the subject of the reputation of the American military, often deliberately and unfairly smeared to benefit anti-American motives, I offer the personal testament of a current British soldier, soon returning to Afghanistan. While having the honour of meeting this gentleman as he holidayed in Australia, I spoke with him about the ongoing efforts in Afghanistan. He spoke of the American troops with veneration to the point where he suggested to me that despite being armed with weaponry and protection, it was only when American troops arrived at a base or were close by, that he felt 'safe'. According to this seasoned officer of the British army, the arrival of US troops marks a "huge sigh of relief". He went on to say that, unlike his own nation's army, and others, the Americans were aggressive, confident, inspirational, and clearly in charge, not limited by paperwork or rules or regulations. It should be remembered that American troops, as well as those of its coalition partners, are the only troops that civilians in these countries actually approach for help or handouts, as opposed to cowering inside in fear of being seen.

Travelling through America, and meeting industry leaders in elite circles, I observed the military precision with which they conducted their work and lives. It was an ethic centred on ensuring maximum use of time, multi-tasking, concentration, strategy and scheduling. On a simple level, given the prevalence of the military in the United States, it is true that many people in elite circles were former military personnel. The core discipline, mental strength, strategy, acumen, and aggression of the military are clearly reflected in the individuals that inhabit these circles and their work.

In America, the military is seen as the protector and purveyor of freedom. This links the most pivotal value with one of the most potent cultural influences, and the combination delivers an impregnable fortress of confidence, gratitude, passion, and faith. There are constant reminders of the continual fight for and pursuit of freedom through countless military cemeteries, school education, tributes, artefacts, museums and memorials dedicated to US participation in war. This commitment to the military also manifests in the glorification of veterans and military history. Much like religion, the military is omnipresent. Stickers on the back windows of cars declaring "Former US Army" or "US Army Veteran", as well as the everyday people wearing caps with "Marines" emblazoned, or t-shirts with the words "Military" or "God Bless Our Troops", attest to this.

An example of this deep-seated commitment came from a Korean veteran I met in Florida. He was in the process of making his funeral and burial arrangements. He and his wife went to the local veteran's cemetery and arranged for what needed to be done upon his death. He asked what the charge was for the space for him and his wife. The answer was: "You've already paid for it."

Many of the older generation express concern that the history of the struggle for freedom in America is becoming lost to members of the younger generation. There are strong parallels to the similar concerns regarding patriotism and, again, I would suggest that, comparatively, young people's appreciation of freedom and its history is still far greater in America than in any other nation on earth. In a country and culture such as America, it is inescapable.

In today's world, a discussion of America's military cannot avoid Guantanamo Bay. To me, personally, it is of little interest. Why the world is so concerned about a small number of radical international terrorists from very unpleasant parts of the world who detest the West is beyond me. Instead of directing their efforts at removing the enablers of modern day Islamic terrorism, such as the bloated welfare systems of every Western country except America, political correctness, and cultural relativism, they seek to direct a political media campaign about American torture. And they have done a masterful job, with even some of America's most ardent supporters suggesting that the existence of and practices at Guantanamo Bay are indefensible.

The purpose of Guantanamo Bay is to prevent enemy combatants from inflicting harm in the future. The context is warfare and, while some may have forgotten, it was an act of war that saw the epoch start on September 11, 2001. The realities of Guantanamo Bay have been hidden by the clever campaign waged domestically and internationally by anti-American forces. It is conveniently overlooked that prisoners receive a complimentary copy of the Koran, that US guards wear gloves when handing the copies out, as the detainees believe US guards are unclean, and that several independent overseas organisations which have visited have declared the facility clean, modern, and well run.

Depicting the US military as 'thuggish brutes' through several allegations of torture at both Guantanamo Bay and Abu Ghraib, including the admission of former President George W. Bush that the mastermind of the September 11th attacks was 'waterboarded' is simply naïve and dangerous. In the face of these matters, the anti-America collective is quick to accuse the United States of hypocrisy in their value system, their freedom identity, and their religiosity. Taking the required action to protect a country's citizens from mass acts of terrorism is not a violation of its moral values. It is the opposite. There is nothing more moral than keeping America strong. If the choice is between civilized restraint and the West's survival, no government or country leader should hesitate. America does not—and all credit to them. War is not the place for compromise. Bad things happen in war. That is a reality. Winston Churchill, the great wartime Prime Minister of England, showed throughout the Second World War that he would always put his nation's people first, with the bombing of innocent Lübeck purely for the purpose of damaging German morale, his plans to use mustard gas in the event of a German invasion, and his attitude toward Mahatma Gandhi's hunger strike in 1943. The actions of the former Bush administration may have been unpleasant, but they were necessary.

It would also be remiss to not discuss humanitarian aid in this chapter. The enormous humanitarian aid programme of the United States is one of the least acknowledged aspects of its role in the world. The enormity of finances and scope of aid is breathtaking. Food, clothes, shelter, and essential supplies are delivered around the world. The military plays a significant role in humanitarian aid through the use of its resources to implement the programmes through delivery and on-the-ground assistance. The humanitarian response of the United States to international disasters has always been substantial, as it understands that with great power comes great responsibility, and because it is a values-driven country. These contributions are largely ignored because they are inconvenient and incompatible with the anti-American agenda worldwide. One need only look at the incredible humanitarian effort of the United States in response to the cataclysmic 2010 Haiti earthquake and its aftermath. Two former United States Presidents are still engaged in humanitarian efforts in Haiti, many months after the event. Another stunning example of American humanitarianism was the aid they provided to Iran in late 2003 in the wake of a deadly earthquake — to a country, many of whose citizens daily pray for America's downfall. Additionally, no greater evidence can be offered of this than former President George W. Bush and his administration's efforts in AIDS assistance in Africa. Irrespective of political views of the Bush administration, this was a tremendous humanitarian effort, unparalleled in world history and, to this day, that administration receives no kudos for it. Neither should we forget the American humanitarian response to the Indonesian tsunami in December 2004. What lends the American humanitarian aid contribution even greater credibility is that it does not chest-thump or publicise its contributions, as do other countries. It does its work quietly and without fuss.

It should also be noted that the United States has come to the aid of countries and people worldwide the moment there is a problem, disaster, or tragedy. Indeed, in the vast majority of instances, the first responder is the United States. One need only look at the tragedy of the crash into the Atlantic Ocean of Air France Flight 447 in June 2009, killing all 228 people on board. The first nation France turned to immediately after the crash was America, asking to use America's unique, state-of-the-art satellite equipment. Consider the context. It was a flight from Brazil to France. The accident was the worst in French aviation history. France has been the most outspoken anti-American nation in the Western world, with anti-Americanism almost stamped in the modern Frenchman's DNA. What did the Americans do? Not only did they allow the French use of their satellites, but even deployed US military personnel to participate in the search and possible rescue effort. US maritime surveillance aircraft with anti-submarine capabilities and patrol aircraft were used in the effort. Such is the soul of the American nation. But they do not seek, nor receive, in countless examples, any level of gratitude.

The military of the United States not only protects and defends the United States and its immediate allies, it protects the world. Its fearsome status and ability to play this role comes from decades of unparalleled military spending by many successive American administrations. For European nations, in particular, the might of the US military, and their protection of these nations, limits the financial burden for these countries in their own defence spending. While the US makes sure the people of these nations sleep at night, the governments of these very nations use the money they thus save to win elections by buying votes through the delivery of lavish social benefits. Yet, supposedly, America epitomise a selfish and imperial foreign policy. America must remember it is a sovereign nation and not let itself be bullied by foreign bodies. About those who believe that military action without the 'consensus of the world' is a display of heartless immorality, I say to America: It is moral to protect your liberty from the unwelcome intrusion of foreign bodies. It might not rate a mention, but Americans have human rights, too.

The truth is this: The world has benefited from American stewardship and leadership, and America is a light on an often dark world. The military plays an intrinsic role in this. The world often forgets the crucial role the United States Department of Defense played in developing the technology of the Internet that is used around the world today—or their creation of the Global Positioning System (GPS) in 1973, a system that now fits so many cars around the world—and has enhanced scientific and technological research as well as the lives of everyday people.

I close this chapter with a recounting of the most moving experience of my entire stay in America. I was able not only to visit the Arlington Cemetery as a tourist, but also had the distinction of visiting with the widow of a decorated soldier who buried her husband there. As I took my first glance around the cemetery, I was taken by its sheer size. In row after row lay America's finest, in one of the most aesthetically beautiful places I had ever seen. While the Tomb of the Unknown Soldier, manned around the clock, was sobering and extraordinarily impressive, it was a private observation that reduced me to tears. As we drove on one of the roads through the cemetery, I observed a man lying on his side facing a grave, with a flimsy fold out chair, pouring water around the flowers on his son's grave, sobbing uncontrollably. It was a middle-aged father visiting his lost son. A heart-wrenching experience, it was such a powerful reminder of the price of spreading freedom. What a price we pay for freedom. America has an uncommon valour.

American troops are God's troops. God Bless America.

A CULTURE OF EXCEPTIONALISM

The whole life of an American is passed like a game of chance, a revolutionary crisis, or a battle.

~Alexis de Tocqueville, *Democracy in America*

AN EXCEPTIONAL CULTURE defines the United States of America.

It is a culture unlike any other on this planet. It is open, buoyant, bold and exciting. It embraces success and audacity. It celebrates eccentricity and demonises mediocrity. It focuses on the individual, not the collective. It promotes fierce competition. It possesses an air of confidence. It breathes an entrepreneurial spirit.

The American culture is the greatest culture in the world today. This is why the rest of the world takes its cue from America. It explains why it is home to the best and brightest of every industry or field. It is also the reason why nations around the world lose their talented and ambitious every day to the United States. It is where the best and talented are nurtured, mentored, guided, promoted, and rise to the top. It is the country where you have the most opportunity to live out a dream or fulfil an ambition.

This all begs the all important question: What is the appeal of the American culture? Before attempting to answer that, remember that the generalist culture we are now discussing is firmly underpinned by the culture of values canvassed in earlier chapters. This grounding provides the vehicle for the ultimate objective of the American — fulfilling dreams through opportunity and risk. In other Western cultures (the closest comparison in cultural terms), the central attitude of the culture is one that consigns the people of those cultures to obscurity. Leading pleasant and contented lives, characterised by conservative small steps, such cultures and their people leave no lasting legacy. The Americans have the correct view of life: that they are the music makers, the dreamers of dreams, and that the only pursuit worthwhile is the seemingly impossible.

It may surprise Americans to learn that in many Western cultures, in countries extremely similar to their own, successful people are criticised, resented, and targeted. These cultures do not like or reward people whose talent or achievements distinguish them. Instead, in these countries, such people are often unfairly sought out to be punished, and every effort is made to take away their confidence by clipping their wings and cutting them down to size. As a result, unlike in America, there is no great incentive to achieve, be inspired, or seize opportunity. People in these cultures become ashamed of their own success. In America, envy is replaced by great admiration, respect, and personal ambition. This is why America loves winners. It loves success. It is the best place in the world to be successful. In America, you are not just spared being cut down; instead, Americans give their utmost to lift you up in any and every way possible. American culture breeds success. It pays to be the best in America.

Consider this true story. An extraordinarily wealthy self-made senior politician in Australia makes an appearance in the annual rich list published by the leading publication in business and industry. This senior politician disputes the propriety of his presence on the list, declares it 'wishful thinking', and claims that a rival politician has more money than he does. Contrast this with the story of a well-known American business magnate. The equivalent publication in the United States dares to suggest that this businessman publicly overstates his wealth, and publishes what it regards as a more accurate figure. The very next day that businessman files numerous lawsuits in courts all over the country, claiming that he is wealthier than what was published, that his reputation has been damaged, and that he is owed an apology. This highlights the reality of cultural differences between America and other English-speaking countries, and the entire Western world, better than any other example.

In America, dreams are dared to be spoken of. Unlike other cultures, where talk of hope and optimism is equated with delusion, and the proponents of such talk are ridiculed as fantasists out of sync with reality, American culture places the concept of 'dreaming' on a pedestal. So prevalent is dreaming in this culture that any person who does not harbour a grand vision for his or her life is demonised. Where its Western counterparts have a culture that strives for mediocrity, America stands proud and strives to be the best. Negativity and mediocrity have no place in America.

Love of the underdog is palpable in American society. As imaginary as Hollywood films may be, this love is reflected in its production of countless inspirational sports stories. Consider the most famous sports story in the history of filmmaking: Rocky. The Rocky story resonates because it is the embodiment of the American dream. Many might feel it is a little rich to categorise a passion for the underdog as uniquely American, but consider this: Other

Western cultures might appear to support the underdog, but the support and love is conditional upon whether the underdog wins. It is not about the journey of the underdog. America's love of the underdog is much more legitimate.

Again, I return to Rocky: In the original film, Rocky loses his fight with Apollo Creed by decision, yet this is entirely brushed over as it is Rocky's journey that is considered to count. In America, so long as you give it your best shot, the outcome is immaterial. Take a real life illustration from Australia of this conditional underdog support syndrome. Jessica Watson, at the age of fifteen, decided she wanted to become the youngest person to sail non-stop, solo and unassisted, around the world. The odds, for obvious reasons, were stacked against her. In October 2009, at the age of sixteen, she set off on her adventure. Prior to her adventure, criticism of her plans, her parents, her family, her experience and her age were widely promoted in the Australian 'commentariat' and in the yachting industry. Talk radio was awash with everyday Australians' fervent criticism, even with calls for the government to step in and refuse to sanction her departure. What happened? Jessica Watson arrived safely back in May 2010, becoming the youngest ever person to circumnavigate the globe unassisted. She did it. Her reception upon arrival to Sydney Harbour was extraordinary. All free-to-air television stations ran all-day live coverage of the event. A huge flotilla of boats met her as she first entered the Harbour. A customised pink carpet had been made for the occasion and thousands of everyday Australians turned out to welcome back 'our Jess' in a spectacular homecoming. Even the Prime Minister was there to greet her and labelled her a new Australian 'hero'. Talk radio was flooded with compliments and talk of how proud it was to be an Australian on this day. This example reinforces the difference in cultural appreciation between America and other Western countries. Some other countries may love winners, but only after they've won. They are not there for the whole journey. The support or rewarding of courage and risk-taking is not there before a positive result. Underdogs or winners have to prove themselves first.

Inspiration defines American culture. Perusing countless bookstores across America, I was struck by the popularity, size, and prominence of the self-help section. Bookstores in America are awash with autobiographies, biographies, and motivational materials. Reading about and learning from someone who you perceive to be the best and greatly admire is a very American concept, and entirely compatible with America's love for and celebration of the successful. Inspiration emboldens a people. From inspiration emerges an audacity and a willingness to take risks. This is intrinsic to success — the need to be challenged. Without risk, man cannot flourish. The greatest strength of American culture is that it encourages, supports, and rewards people willing to take risks. The Declaration of Independence specifically enshrines the right of every American to pursue his or her happiness, and this right continues to be protected every day by the cultural attitude toward risk.

With inspiration also comes enormous emotion. If the psyche of individuals or communities is susceptible to inspiration and dreams, they are, by default, susceptible to great emotion. Without doubt, the most emotional culture in the world is the American. Americans are moved by personal stories of people and journeys of triumph in the face of great adversity. Speaking for the first time in front of audiences all over the United States, I had to accustom myself to audience members impulsively calling out "That's right", "Exactly", "Yes, sir", and "God Bless

America". As noted in an earlier chapter, it is not uncommon to see audience members silently crying or gyrating gently. Non-Americas no doubt consider this as typical American overkill but they fail to realise that this emotion is the source of America's strength and allows it to be the greatest country in the world.

The culture is a very inclusive one. Scepticism and suspicion are not instant emotions or first reactions. Americans will accept you on face value; there are no preconceptions with the American people. Only where these conditions exist, can a country claim to be the land of opportunity. Many other countries' peoples pride themselves on the ability to identify swindle and disingenuousness. This may be a wonderful defence mechanism for the dishonest few, but such a protective wall limits the opportunities of the many. All are initially subjected to this protective wall and greeted with its associated irreverence. As a result, many positive forces are eroded and never see fruition. This then fosters an environment of reluctance, where people do not feel that there is sufficient benefit from offering a new idea or being innovative, as negativity and doubt are automatic responses. America has a much more far-sighted and less small-minded approach in which it is prepared to be stung a couple of times as it realises that the reward for such openness and inclusion overall is far too great to be denied.

This is also, coincidentally, a great example of the sentiment toward risk-taking. The greatest reflection of this positivity, confidence, and risk-taking is seen in the way Americans are always talking each other up and vouching for each other— "You've got to meet this guy, a great guy, he's done this, he's done that." Individuals within other Western cultures exercise caution at all times, holding the view that while they might like someone, an automatic transfer of opinion is not guaranteed. In other words, there is an absence of confidence in their own judgement. While this may seem inconsequential, it must be remembered that inspiration is a contagious and permeating influence. Nothing ventured, nothing gained.

Offering novel ideas and different concepts to other Western audiences is particularly difficult due to this defensive reluctance, and it is the reason why many suggest that such cultures reject innovation. Such acts are immediately seized upon by a media and leadership within the country that believe they own the deed to normality and have a monopoly on judgement. Being different by exhibiting individuality and independence in these countries is not the way to get ahead in life. Self-promotion is considered the gravest of sins and the poorest of forms. The contrast could not be starker. Eccentricity and innovation are celebrated in America. Not only are they celebrated, unless you exhibit them, you do not get ahead.

Americans are fascinated by eccentricity and consume it. Take the founder of a new concept as an example. Americans will desire to know how the concept originated and how it formed. Sure, they will test it with questions, but with genuine inquisitiveness, not snarling negativity, incredulity, or an inclination to pooh-pooh it and brand it self-promotion. In America, not only are you not chopped down; Americans actively do their utmost to lift you up. American culture gives everyone his or her shot. Eccentric, brilliant people never really fit in to their environments. If they are in politics, they don't fit into political parties. If they are in sports, they don't fit into their clubs. If they are teachers, they don't fit into their schools. Often, such people deliberately emphasise their eccentricity to further their careers. In cultures such as the ones described, these people are deemed either loonies or troublemakers or people unable to be part of a team. In America, by contrast, these people are not lopped, ostracised, or derided; rather, they are cherished and celebrated, with every opportunity given to them to succeed in their respective fields.

The same way that positive cultures thrive on positivity, negative cultures thrive on negativity. In a negative culture there are many disillusioned and envious people who sit and carp loudly on the sidelines, and to great effect. These people do not have a voice in America, as it is a positive culture, and people are quick to rally around. America loves winners and success. If ever one wanted evidence of how Americans celebrate a successful individual and place him on a pedestal, all one need do is visit Graceland, the former home of Elvis Presley.

Returning to the Declaration of Independence's "pursuit of happiness", we see the birth of the idea of opportunity as intrinsic to the psyche of a nation. True to its form, America does opportunity better than anyone else. From where does the old observation 'Only in America' come? Anything is possible in America because its people are free and its culture is enrobed in the right to pursue happiness. Notice it is not an automatic right to happiness, but to the pursuit of it. Opportunity is what America offers, through its size, population, and culture of desiring and breeding winners.

One example of how the best and brightest are cherished in America is the mentoring culture that exists across all industries and fields. The best indicator of the greatness of a culture is whether that culture allows a country to be visionary and provide capacity for the young, up-and-coming generation to be nurtured and guided. The problem with most cultures around the world is that they are a reflection of decadent humanity, not values. As such, they are inherently selfish and short-sighted. In such cultures, no great weight is given to mentoring. No one takes anyone under a wing because, in these cultures, everyone is supposedly on the same level. A good illustration of this can be seen in the experience of a close friend of mine who, having won the University Medal in his chosen field, was considering an academic career but rejected it on the grounds that despite there being excellent universities, it is practically impossible to obtain a teaching position while undertaking postgraduate study at an Australian university. In fact, both of his Honours supervisors advised him that if he were if serious about pursuing a career in academia, the only practical option would be to undertake study in America, due to the excellence of their mentoring programs. The view from those who might be potential mentors in other countries is: "No one helped me. No one mentored me. Why should I bother? They'll learn. Everyone does." While this would be anathema to Americans, as they would see the greater stakes at play, such as national interest, they must remember that other cultures, so fragmented by the idea of tearing one another down, are unsurprisingly, low on patriotism. There is no view to building for the future. America, on the other hand, looks ahead and spreads its seeds far and wide, ensuring key pro-American individuals are in every country. This is why they will always be one step ahead of everyone else.

For example, the entire notion of writing a letter 'cold' to a leader in the hope of a response or of being given a chance is a very American thing to do. Drawing from both personal experience and the experiences of others, I feel safe in saying that American leaders are not only accommodating, but also eager to meet young people striving for success in their respective industries. Even just learning about how one can become the best by reading a book about the best or by someone who is successful is a very American thing to do. This is what young, aspiring people all around America do. By contrast, in Australia and other Western countries, the only time industry leaders meet industry aspirants is when these aspirants happen to belong to certain demographic groups whose interests the media or government promote as more important than those of the society as a whole.

To give a real life example of the acknowledgement of opportunity, I recount this experience. Catching an early morning shuttle from my Orlando hotel to the airport, I engaged in an interesting conversation with the driver of the shuttle bus. A middle-aged Swiss immigrant who came to America some twenty years earlier, he was interested in knowing why I held America in such high esteem. After informing him of my reasons, he agreed with all of my sentiments and made the point that while he felt that lifestyle and enjoyment of life were greater in Europe, America was the place to be. Referring to the "unfriendly, reserved nature" of Europeans, he said of Europe, "People won't let you do what you want to do there", before declaring America "the land of opportunity".

As mentioned in the introduction to this chapter, except in matters of national interest, the emphasis of the culture is on the individual, not the collective. Descriptions of American society range from the kinder "survival of the fittest" to the less kind "dog-eat-dog". Regardless of the description, the analysis is right, and this is precisely why America is the greatest country in the world. America is a Darwinian society where only the strongest survive. First and foremost, this makes American culture a physical embodiment of reality. There is no second place. This means that competition is everywhere in America, on every level. There is a valedictorian. A star quarterback. Children are raised to understand that they must compete in life and that the emphasis is on being the best. This is, again, vastly different from the politically correct, non-offensive route of education in other places around the world where it is now commonplace for teachers to tell young children after a sports game that despite one team losing, there was no winner. Instead, every person was a winner. In the same way, now no one can fail at school. However, competition is not an evil term; to the contrary, when individuals perform their best there is a collective benefit. If a culture cannot provide for internal competition, how can it expect to compete on the world stage?

Consider this: While travelling through America, I was told a story that exemplified the belief in competition, individuality, and success. In the face of the performance of a brilliant track and field star who had the year before won all seven of the Track and Field events, the local school considered introducing a rule that would allow a competitor to run in only three events. This suggestion was met with huge outrage as it was seen not only to limit the potential for individual success, but also to detract from the quality of the competition. As the person recounting the story said to me: "If this guy was good enough to win them all, so he should. It just means everyone else just has to train and work harder." America is the only country that still promotes competition and calls it the way it is.

The United States is the land of the individual. Only when it comes to its country's affairs does it concentrate on the collective. In business, life, and social development, American culture firmly underlines the individual. In other Western cultures, a vague and undefined concept of 'teamwork' is bandied about. This is an idea that involves each person possessing certain qualities which qualify him to be a 'team player'. The idea is that no one individual is bigger than the organisation of which he or she is a part, that it is better to employ someone with no talent but a team spirit than a brilliant individualist. This can be applied to sports, politics, and corporate offices. This timid and insecure attitude is, not surprisingly, absent in the United States. America is a country where the individual is glorified to the point that he or she becomes the organisation.

Travelling through America, one sees billboards promoting individual personal injury lawyers who belong to larger firms. After proclaiming them the best, the advertising then advises people to call the lawyer, not the firm. Call the person. If you look hard enough, you will see in tiny print the name of the lawyer's firm somewhere in the corner. The reason America rejects the collective theory relates to the performance sub-culture, which is discussed in the next chapter. In American culture, an individual working to his optimum is seen to also generally optimise the collective, and this has the same desired outcome of the timid and insecure cultural sentiment of working as a 'team'. The difference is that it is done in a natural way wherein people are able to independently achieve without being subjected to the moral judgement and uneasiness about their role within a team. The concept of dreaming toward higher aspirations is also an inherently personal act which further makes the case that the Americans have it right.

Analysing more deeply the concept of the individual helps explain why America is exceptional. America's roots are profoundly anti-statist. Sovereignty is invested in the people, not the state. Economic statism is one of the greatest dangers to a culture of exceptionalism. Statists detest personal success and are loath to allow it to be rewarded. For as long as America can reject the statist tendencies that have courted then impregnated the rest of the West, it will remain exceptional.

Perhaps the most frequent criticism of Americans is their lack of humility. The greatest product of the inferior cultures of this world today is this concept of 'humility'. Humility, as a character trait, is greatly overrated, the worst form of conceit. In fact, I would go as far as to say that is not a virtue or an ideal. It only prospers in cultures that do not prize accurate representations of reality. In the real world, the humble and the weak get trodden on. It is the brilliant, talented, and confident—along with the bullies, thugs, criminals—who rule the world. It is a necessity in the real world that is America to promote yourself, call yourself the best, and engender inspiration in others so that they extend to you that ladder of opportunity. In the real world that America is, you must tell people you are the best. The idea in other cultures that such a position is arrogant is incorrect. Extreme confidence and assertiveness—which the Americans rightfully have, as the most powerful people on the earth—is often perceived, erroneously, as arrogance.

A further ground for the superiority of American culture is its attitude toward and emphasis on children. While parents around the world must make their children conscious of discipline and boundaries, it would appear that a greater freedom is afforded to American children by American parents. The focus seems to be on instilling supreme confidence in their children. Observing the behaviour of parents in public toward their small children in America provided an interesting comparison to the equivalent in Australia. I noticed that Americans were prepared to let their kids run off steam, and do what kids do. Often parents would comment about their child's energy, saying, "Look where she's going. Isn't she just a trip?" or see the humorous side of what was occurring. This is different from the attitude of Australian parents who are very quick to chide their child and, in the same sort of situation, sternly call out the child's name repeatedly to get their attention, or physically grab them, bring them back to their side, and proceed to scold them firmly. American lenience is an example of freedom, allowing individuality to flourish and allowing the child to become accustomed to 'performing' in public. In the Australian example, the reaction typifies the collective message: "Kid, keep your head down, behave yourself, be quiet; there are other people here." In other Western democracies, particularly the United Kingdom, there exists a vague concept of being 'inappropriate' (not confined to the example of parent-child relations, in fact used in all walks of life within such countries, but perhaps best exemplified through this example), despite there being little or no consensus on a definition of this concept. Parents in America do not just wish a comfortable life for their children; rather, they want their children to be the best in whatever they do. Preparing them for the competitive, swim-or-sink culture of the United States means parents start training and pressuring their children at a younger age and this, in turn, leads to mental strength and an ability to handle pressure. The increasing prevalence of home schooling in America is an example of the focus of parents on their children.

The consumerist culture of the United States feeds into its cultural presuppositions. Consumption, unlike in other countries, is not limited to products or brands. Every aspect of life is consumed in America. Media, celebrities, speeches, and ideas are areas of where consumption in America is like no other. Such consumption is the reason that so many around the world consider the average American to be stupid. They mistake consumerism and the absence of scepticism in Americans as gullibility and stupidity. What they do not understand or realise is that American culture is a consumerist and opportunity-driven one where people are pursuing happiness and a dream.

A practical example: Many Americans, to the outside world, react to certain media personalities in a much more fervent and passionate way. These people take what such personalities say as gospel. The outside world reaches the obvious conclusion that such people must be devoid of critical intelligence to be so 'taken' by these personalities. This is completely incorrect, and unjustified. It is American culture and emotion at play. Americans view these celebrity personalities as extraordinarily successful, are inspired by them, and aspire be them. In their minds, the best way of setting their life on the right track to achieve this objective is to consume what such personalities say. That is not stupidity; it is hope and optimism and the culture of respecting and wanting to emulate success.

American culture is also unquestionably moulded by the unreserved nature of American personality. In general terms, Americans have a much greater confidence in themselves, and this is reflected in their interactions in the community. They are an extroverted people, assured of their place, eager and willing to express an opinion. Moderation of opinion for the purposes of not offending does not, by and large, exist. This feeds well into the freedom-of-speech value at the core of America that also sees the weakest defamation and libel legislation in the world. Americans are the freest people in the world.

Education in the United States is not limited simply to formal school education. Given the size of the population and the corresponding size of the market, American children have the luxury of being exposed to a prevailing television culture. This television culture is, in my view, the explanation of why it is virtually impossible to find an inarticulate American. Even the most impoverished, uneducated American presents confidently with not just clear, coherent expression, but with individual eloquence as well. Again, this may be an assertion that many Americans might consider inaccurate, but it is an assertion made in comparison of Americans with people all around the world. I was struck by how confident and articulate five year olds are in America, compared to their Western peers. Not only do I believe that education in America is vastly more advanced than in other Western countries, in that it promotes public communication, but also that this formal education is complemented by a pervading television culture. Simply, my theory is that American children are born watching articulate, eloquent, and confident people and, as a result, this way of speaking and presenting becomes second nature. The guy on television speaks like that, so they do, too. They are surrounded by these influences.

While an anti-American agenda has focused the world's attention on other aspects of American culture, it cannot be denied that the American people are a humanitarian and philanthropic one. Philanthropy plays a crucial role in American prosperity. The fact is that the biggest philanthropists in history have come from America. During America's 'Golden Age' the great industrialists and bankers—such as Rockefeller, Vanderbilt, Mellon, Carnegie, Ford, and others—gave birth to American philanthropy, founding some of the enduring philanthropic foundations. In current terms, Bill Gates, Chairman of Microsoft, springs to mind. Gates and his wife lead the world in philanthropy, and their acts have paved the way for significant advances in global health and education.

I also witnessed philanthropy on a smaller scale. In Texas, I had the tremendous fortune of visiting a tiny town called Bastrop, some thirty miles out of Austin. The occasion was an annual rodeo: the 2009 11th Annual Brent Thurman Memorial PBR Bull Riding. Many Americans will be familiar with the tragic story of Brent Thurman, rodeo star and one of the world's best riders who, at the age of twenty-five, was killed in a competition rodeo event in 1994. This event is now, for the last eleven years, held in his honour. I was honoured to be there as a guest after Kay Thurman learned that I am an Australian. Her son, Brent, had visited Australia and, through training with a number of Australians, had had a great many Australian friends. Meeting the mother of Brent Thurman was a truly incredible experience; she was one of those people who inspires you just with her presence. An amazing and inspirational lady, Kay Thurman, is still obviously touched by the tragic events of fifteen years ago. She now dedicates her life to helping less fortunate, intellectually and physically challenged children by holding this event to raise money for them.

That Americans are a humanitarian people and that American community spirit is stronger than ever can not be better evidenced than by the restoration efforts in New Orleans after Hurricane Katrina, which are still ongoing to this day. I was hosted by the President of the St Bernard's Parish, a parish southeast of New Orleans, in a visit to the Parish offices. It was one of the parishes worst affected by Hurricane Katrina, with its current population now only half of what it was in 2005. Having been given a personal tour of the devastation to both the city of New Orleans and the parish, I was invited to join the Parish President to address a group of high school student volunteers from the state of Illinois. These American teenagers were sacrificing their own summer vacation to come and help restoration efforts within the Parish. I was moved as I saw these teenagers at the end of their stay, visibly tired, many covered in paint and other house materials, sit and be graciously thanked for their efforts. When the Parish President opened up the floor for casual questions, I was struck by the quality and perceptiveness of questions asked by these students and by their deep concern about the impact of Katrina on the Parish and the state of Louisiana in general.

Finally, the culture of America is the culture of values. When the anti-American agenda attacks America on any number of issues, the underlying attack is on culture. For as long as America remains true to her values and principles and to her Constitution and the Declaration of Independence, the United States will forever reign.

The culture war is the whole ballgame. If we lose it, there is not another America to pull us out.

BUSINESS AND CONSUMERISM

As one digs deeper into the national character of the Americans,
one sees that they have sought the value of everything
in this world only in the answer to this single question:
How much money will it bring in?

~Alexis de Tocqueville, *Democracy in America*

AN ANALYSIS OF BUSINESS AND CONSUMERISM in the United States is a most valuable exercise in unlocking the American psyche. There are several reasons for this. First and foremost is the economic might from which America derives so much of its success and power; second is the eminence of consumerism in America; and third is the role business has in the culture of opportunity and the pursuit of happiness. This is not to mention the world perspective: The greatest accomplishment of America is spreading American culture around the world, and American business is pivotal to this objective.

In my travels, I was fortunate to experience firsthand the ordinary American perspective on work, and the absolute depth and size of some American business. Of note, in Central Illinois, in the town of Bloomington, I was given a tour of the grounds of the headquarters of State

Farm Insurance, the largest home and automobile insurer in America. In the next town, named Normal, I was blown away by the sheer size of the Mitsubishi plant, the company's only North American plant, with a capacity for 240,000 cars per year. The local employment these two companies alone provide is staggering.

Quite simply, two interconnected concepts are the reason American business, industry, and economy are without peer: performance culture and competition. Capitalism and entrepreneurial innovation are values firmly ingrained in American history, and they imbue the belief in its future. These values are remarkably compatible with the two most important documents of the United States—the Declaration of Independence and the Constitution—which compatibility further evidences the extraordinary vision of the founding fathers. It is true also that, historically, great care has been taken to protect the entrepreneurial capacity of business.

This is one of the many reasons that, rightly or wrongly, America is a considered the greatest place on earth to do business. The general perception of entrepreneurs and business owners in other countries around the world is that the climate in America for business is far friendlier than in their own countries. They point to the ease of doing business, the ease of attaining capital, the fact that it is not cost-prohibitive. They find limited red tape, greater support for business owners, and industrial relations legislation inclined toward the employer as a result of a weaker union influence.

Take for example, the giant retailer Walmart, to which I will return later in the chapter. As far as business success is concerned, Walmart is difficult to look past. Onerous and cumbersome bureaucracy and planning laws meant that its plans for expansion to Europe were greatly thwarted, as they could not set up their type of superstore. Likewise, their German experiment showed that German law was totally incompatible with the successful Walmart culture and Statement of Ethics, which forbids intimate relationships between employees. Again, the difference between the relationship of government and business in America and the equivalent relationship in other countries is stark and shows why the world clamours to do business in America.

More than that, many non-American entrepreneurs around the world yearn to have the opportunity to participate in a business culture that is considered the ultimate litmus test of the success of a business. With the sheer size of the market, a result of the American blessing of its large population (which translates to no shortage of both workers and consumers), comes ever-expanding competition in business threatening the leader across every industry. The equation is simple: Greater competition leads to even greater business, which leads to American exceptionalism in the private sector. In the face of greater competition and continual threats, a business or company is forced to rediscover, revitalise, re-imagine, and remake. Innovation becomes intrinsic to the conduct of business. Persistent competition, coupled with the culture's overarching Darwinian 'survival of the fittest' ethic, makes corporate and capitalist America the fiercest and greatest in the world.

Let us not forget: Americans invented the steamboat, the telegraph, the steel plow, the reaper, the telephone, the phonograph and the assembly line—to mention just a few. Unprecedented innovation has lead to unprecedented wealth.

While consumerism is not a concept exclusive to the United States by any stretch, no one 'does' consumerism like the United States. The culture of buying and spending, often more than the consumers earn, is unparalleled. The easy way that the American people latch onto a business name and concept is like no where else in the world. In America, a business name is linked to a product. For example, it's Starbucks, not coffee. It's Ben & Jerry's, not ice cream. The streets of New York are lined with men and women selling novel products and with Americans purchasing them. On Beale Street in Memphis, a six-year-old African-American boy is collecting a small fortune in a bin through performing tumble turns. In small towns in Pennsylvania, even the Amish people exhibit a true entrepreneurial spirit, with furniture, grocery and produce stores. Consumerism requires entrepreneurship. In America, both are everywhere; they are intrinsic to the culture. Nor is the success just in America. Visiting the 'World of Coca-Cola' in Atlanta and reviewing the history of the product was a telling experience. Coca-Cola is sold now in over two hundred countries in the world. McDonalds has more than thirty thousand restaurants worldwide. Hollywood receives more than half of its revenue outside the US. These giant brands are a big support to American soft power around the world, and signify the importance of the health of American business to its identity.

The majority of business concepts that now are part and parcel of business and trade across the world were born in the United States. Take for example the service ethos. Many American businesses have set the service ethos that the world has come to expect and that many businesses around the world have adopted. A small example of the innovative execution of this ever-improving service offering that is now imitated around the world was started by Wal-Mart (as it was then known): a greeter placed at the door, with the sole duty of pointing customers in the right direction. This tenet of personalisation of service is now integral to most companies' service policies for employees. However, service ethos and selling strategy can also come together in a unique link of business and psychology for much more powerful effect. American minds had the foresight to identify the potential of great service and this led to the birth of up-selling and/or cross-selling, two selling strategies. The slogan of Rotary is useful in such an analysis: "Service above Self" and its adage "He profits most who serves best." It is that attitude that the best entrepreneurs follow. These strategies have influenced the sale of goods, and without them, many businesses would not survive.

Americans also continue to lead the business world in motivation — as a business concept — for employees. This concept, still in its infancy, has been well received by employees in its implementation. The key asset of the United States in this important area is that its general culture is conducive to motivation, and to employees receiving praise from superiors in the spirit in which it is offered. As discussed in the previous chapter, it is the case that Americans respect success and that the presence of this attitude in the workplace means employees have a much greater respect for their superiors, which, in turn, means that praise and motivation can engender a much better relationship.

Consider this: Every morning, in every Walmart store across the United States, employees gather together and are led in a cheer by the Store Manager: "Give me a 'W'. Give me an 'A'. Give me an 'L' ...", etc. until a crescendo is reached at "W A L M A R T!" Such acts are tremendously powerful in employee retention, loyalty, and workplace atmosphere. It is interesting to see an act we usually associate with support of a sporting team used in the formal workplace, but this is yet another example of American flamboyance, confidence, brilliance, and eccentricity. Again, such an exercise is possible only in a culture where people are unreserved and passionate. It is difficult to imagine this exercise being successful in the reserved cultures of other Western countries, for example. This Walmart practice represents a strong trait of American culture. It is also one of the reasons why Walmart is the largest company in world history and is emblematic of American greatness in the world. Walking into Walmarts across America, one is immediately moved by the sheer size, scope, organization, and service offered. When one considers that it all began in tiny Bentonville, Arkansas as Walton's Five and Dime, it is a truly uplifting story.

Management within business is another area essential to any discourse on business. Critics of the United States suggest that it is incapable of fostering positive relations in the world outside its own confines. This is as absurd as it is offensive when considering the fact that American executives of American companies employ citizens all over the world and keep those employees loyal and motivated. Similarly, the same critics are quick to cast aspersions on the capitalist spirit of America, but they overlook how much wealth and health this spirit has brought the world. A simple but powerful example is the business method of franchising. America is the home of the franchise, overseeing its introduction and successful implementation. This concept has enabled people around the world to become small business owners and has, in turn, spread the values of freedom and liberty and given countless people the opportunity to pursue happiness. It appears America can do no wrong; even its internal weaknesses appear to strengthen the world.

No greater evidence of this exists than the litigious society that America has now become. As a result of this, America has, in the business world, developed the strongest OHS standards, operational programs, and staff training. In short, this means that workplaces around the world are safer places.

On the topic of the influence of American business in the world, remember this: Business success equates to financial freedom and the realisation of dreams. The dream of a two- story house, two kids, two cars, and a dog began in the United States. Today across the world, many people have attained this dream. Through America spreading the values of freedom and capitalism, it has given people the chance to fulfil this dream.

Much like its people, American businesses have an unquenchable desire to be the best. Self-promotion is a necessary norm and, much like everything else, the vehicle for this promotion is continuous innovation and improvement. As a result, it is unsurprising that there exists a very clear performance culture. This performance culture is key to American exceptionalism and the reason for America leading in virtually every industry. The American workplace may not be perfect, but it is closer to a meritocracy than anywhere else in the world. Unlike in many Western countries, the correct social connections, nepotism, and currying personal favour with the boss are immaterial. In the fierce, highly charged world that is American business, the only thing that counts is performance; a business simply cannot afford a mediocre employee. In a similar vein, aggression defines the American workplace, with ambition made public and vying for promotion done openly. This is in stark contrast to more reserved Western cultures where it is considered poor form to pursue a promotion openly, and one must wait patiently to be 'tapped on the shoulder'. This returns us to the idea of competition. The American business world rewards entrepreneurial activity. Employers actively encourage their employees to display entrepreneurial flair. There is an active culture within business to encourage people to be the best. In Burger Kings and other restaurants all around America, an 'Employee of the Month' plaque hangs. I was greatly amused to see, in almost every one of the locations I visited in the United States, eateries variously proclaiming: "World's greatest hamburger", "World's best pasta", "World's most famous hot dogs". Often identical mantles would be claimed on the same street by three or four restaurants. This is a reflection of the competitive nature of American business—a wonderful element which forces eateries to continually improve their food and service, making them the best they can be. It is also a reflection of American confidence in their claiming of "World" status— the same attitude that has seen them reach unassailable heights.

On just my second day in America, I met in Las Vegas a California woman who was celebrating her birthday and coincidental promotion. A single mum in her early twenties, she worked in the real estate industry back home. Over dinner, she passionately outlined her views about striving for perfection and having purpose in life and articulated her desire to be the best, and her dislike of laziness or mediocrity. She told me that she fought every month, without fail, to be the most successful realtor. She recounted a story: One of her bosses had told her it was impossible for her to have six months in succession as the most successful realtor. She told me she used this as the ultimate motivation to prove the boss wrong, and she ended up being the top listing agent from 2007-2009, and employee of the year for 2008-2009. The open discussion of unbridled ambition in the context of life philosophy was incredibly refreshing, and something that I had seldom experienced in my travels in the world before. I remember thinking at the time that if this is the attitude of young Americans, America's future is sound.

In my travels through the United States, I had the tremendous fortune of witnessing the ingenuity of the private sector firsthand. I toured the Beistle Company in Shippensburg, Pennsylvania. The Beistle Company recently celebrated its one hundred and tenth birthday and holds the distinction of being the oldest and biggest party manufacturing company in the world. A producer of hats, napkins, confetti, stickers, wall-clings, and all party paraphernalia, and a distributor to hospitals, military, and schools, its scope is enormous. A family-run company, it has endured and is a story typical of American spirit. While all of its competitors moved their manufacturing to China, Beistle made a commitment to protect American jobs and said simply that it would operate with exceptional efficiencies to compete with China. Its employee turnover rate is extremely low. Employing some two hundred and fifty employees, with a combined facility size of 900,000 square feet (inclusive of office, factory and distribution centre), its size is breathtaking. The ingenuity of the engineers who designed the complex machines is astounding. The care taken by employees to ensure the absence of fault in all products, by individually assessing each, symbolises American excellence in quality.

To get an idea of just how deeply the performance culture is embedded in the American culture and psyche, one need only look at the custom of tipping. The United States is the only country in the world where tipping is a fundamentally integrated aspect of the economy — that is to say, where employees must rely on tips to make ends meet, the economy is engineered to have low hourly rates, and tipping is automatic and virtually compulsory. This is yet another example of the incentives of performance and a desire to be the best. It literally pays to be the best. Waitresses in New York earn just two dollars fifty an hour. Without tips, they could not survive. The logic is: the better the service, the bigger the tip. Travel in a taxi, or receive service from a waiter at a restaurant in America and chances are such people go to great lengths to be helpful and polite and to provide you with the best experience. The process of tipping also differentiates the private sector and a government job—an important demarcation that lends greater strength and scope to the private sector but is not necessarily seized upon by other countries' private sectors. As has been discussed throughout this book, America is a very humanitarian country through its values, and tipping is another example of this. Every time a customer provides a tip, he or she is reminded of the need to look after others in the community. There is no better engagement of the community spirit of looking after each other, which typifies America.

The support of education and the role of universities in American exceptionalism should also not be discounted. The stories of Google, Microsoft, Facebook and Hewlett Packard all began in the computer labs of universities in America with the brilliance of young entrepreneurs. The role of Stanford University in the story of Google is particularly heart-warming, with its financial investment stake in Google and the continual encouragement and support by university administration and staff. It is difficult to imagine other universities in other countries within the confines of cultures that strive for mediocrity investing so much belief in such projects. It was with great interest that I had the chance to tour Hamburger University, the training facility of McDonalds Corporation, located in Oak Brook, Illinois. An entire university covering eighty acres of land is dedicated to training McDonald's personnel, and teaches people from more than a hundred and nineteen countries. This type of institution would only ever be found in America.

The American ideal of opportunity also finds its manifestation within the business world and its treatment of extremely successful entrepreneurs. It is not rare to see or read about such American entrepreneurs at some point making a bad business decision and failing, becoming bankrupt, only to then again reach dizzy heights of success. In fact, such stories are celebrated. This underscores the culture of opportunity in America. In America, it is easy to redeem yourself from mistakes or failures, and quickly return to public favour. Americans adore the comeback story and the underdog. Mistakes and failings do not permanently damage or tarnish one's reputation, unlike the unforgiving cultures of other Western countries. America truly is the country of unlimited chances.

One final thought: This is not to say that America's predisposition for risk is always rewarded. Both the Great Depression of 1929 and the Financial Crisis of 2008 began in America. However, this should not be seen as evidence of anything inherently rotten in the American economy. When compared with the economic growth of the 1990s and 2000s, such temporary dislocation, from which America always recovers, seems to have been worth it in the long run. It has always been the American way that adversity brings out the best in its people and culture. From early defeats by Britain in the War of Independence, to the days following Pearl Harbor, to the loss of the Philippines, to the recession of the 1980s, America has always emerged stronger than before. I predict a similar outcome to the current Financial Crisis, dubbed as the second Great Depression of our time.

DEMOCRACY AND POLITICS

*America is a place where anyone can grow up and become
the President of the United States.*

Old Adage

INSPIRATION, INDEPENDENCE, AND OPPORTUNITY characterise
politics and democracy in the United States. As such, the
American democratic and political system is the ultimate
manifestation of American culture – specifically
performance culture. While admittedly not perfect, the
United States has the *most perfect* form of democracy in the
world. It is a rigorous meritocracy that rewards talent,
performance and risk-taking.

I must warn that democracy and politics is one of those
areas where, based on individual experience, some people
hold opinions which will contradict the sentiments
expressed in this chapter. It is important to remember that
the ensuing analysis is general and that it compares the
American to other systems.

It is difficult for Americans to appreciate the talent of
their elected representatives or to recognise that the process
of nomination and election is entirely premised on merit, as
they would probably not be well versed in the political

landscapes of other countries. It might surprise them if they knew. It would be futile to compare American politics and democracy with the systems of countries like China or Zimbabwe. For the purposes of fair comparison, we will draw upon America's cousins, Australia and Britain.

Australia's political system is a robotic machine where a convergence of ideas set by a few key individuals determines the tone for the country. Within this culture, political party nominations for Parliamentary seats mostly result in political hacks with little life experience, and the emphasis is on loyal service to the political party, as opposed to talent, charisma and ability. Similarly, but perhaps more sinisterly, there is the notion of 'party discipline': If an elected representative in the Parliament or local Council has the endorsement of a political party, there is a concept of 'ownership' of that individual by that party. Not supporting every policy position of the party is not an option.

Herein lies one of the chief problems associated with Australian political discourse—the tendency to ignore the fact that people affiliated with a political party are individuals. Instead, everything is viewed as one monolithic block. What one or two members do is taken to reflect on the whole party. If any one individual, no matter how minor, does not toe the line, he is made a scapegoat and his views are attributed by the media and other critics to the party as a whole.

Such an approach is not only logically unsound, it also stifles democratic debate. On both sides of the Australian political sphere, elected representatives are too afraid to comment for fear of their thoughts being assigned to the party, from which criticism would ensue. Such a mindset can hardly be good for democracy. Similarly, the Australian media's obsession with persecuting anyone outside what they consider the 'norm' of politics is also harmful for the Australian system of government. With a media culture obsessed with attacking anyone who shows personality traits that indicate individuality, it is not surprising that Australian confidence in government is low. The Australian media force politicians to conform to a standard no human could ever aspire to. In sum, Australia has a stagnant political mould incapable of inspiration, independence, or opportunity.

Take for example, conservatism. Unlike in the United States, the conservative movement in Australia is in its infancy in terms of being a movement based upon ideas and principles. Instead, Australia has a movement that is centred on party politics, whereby the Liberal Party (which, despite its name, is the party of conservative politics) accommodates a 'broad church' philosophy. Thus it encompasses conservatives, libertarians, quasi-democratic-socialists, and moderate liberals as one. This conglomeration creates a bastardisation of ideas, wherein compromise is the way of the day, and true conservative thought is diluted in a hodgepodge of less-than-centre-right ideas. The same is true of politics on the left side of the spectrum.

It should be remembered that the above describes the political landscape of the country closest to America in values, history, and freedoms, yet it has an astonishingly inferior political and democratic system. Consider this: When an MP (Member of Parliament) in the Westminster system—the system of Britain and Australia—'crosses the floor' to vote against his party's position, it is a crisis. In the United States, it is just another day. This is because, much like its values-based culture, the emphasis in America is centred on independence, risk-taking, the individual, independent thought, and the theory of merit.

Independence in British and Australian politics is therefore virtually non-existent; anyone who has his own mind and speaks out is instantly branded a cowboy or a rogue, or derided as 'not a team player'. Again, unlike in America, the rest of the world focuses on the collective, not the individual. America is even more greatly unique in that, despite such emphasis, it demonstrates greater capacity than those 'collective-centric' countries to summon all individuals into an amazingly powerful collective.

An illustration of the weight given to freedom, opportunity, and merit in the political system of America is the fact that any citizen of any state can run for any office anywhere in the country, provided that he moves into the jurisdiction and officially changes his residency to there. Picture an aspiring politician born, bred, and living in North Dakota, with limited opportunity in his home state. In America, he has the freedom and opportunity to run for office in Florida, for example. More than this freedom, the culture of merit in the political system ensures that his bid is not poisoned from the outset. Americans are not a small-minded people; their eye is always firmly fastened on the greater cause. Is he the best man for the job? Do his credentials and experience qualify him for office? To Americans, unlike the Australians and British, familiarity and service with and to the local area is only one minor consideration. In the Australian or British system, if someone dares to seek to represent an area with which he has only limited connection, if the pre-selection committee does not put a stop to the candidacy, parochial constituencies will certainly do so on election day.

No nation on earth other than the United States engages in the process of primary elections. Instead, in most countries, a small, select group of people from the party, including senior Party bureaucrats, meet to determine the fate of a prospective candidate. This process is called 'pre-selection' in Australia and 'selection' in Britain. This effectively removes the opportunity of an individual to control his own destiny or, at the very least, to allow the populace to make their judgement on a candidate. America's primary system gives everyone an opportunity to prove why he or she is the best person for the job.

To return to the earlier example of the North Dakotan seeking office in Florida: the primary system provides him with the chance to go to the people and plead his case. The equivalent of primary election — the pre-selection/selection process used in Australian and British political systems — comprises a small committee of dedicated party people who invariably are aligned to a party faction. Capacity to win an election is outweighed by service to the party and previous support of other party candidates. Forget for one moment the effect of this on the quality of those who enter public service or the consequences of this for a nation's future. Most importantly, what does this say about the Western principle of democracy, as opposed to the American? It sounds repetitive, but it's true: As with everything else, no one does democracy like America.

Americans love democracy. They elect state, federal, county, and town council representatives. Almost yearly, they vote on propositions, elect school boards, funeral boards, sanitation officers, sheriffs, and everything up to the town's dog catcher. In other Western nations, these positions are filled by the bureaucracy: the police force, local schools, town planning, hospitals, cemeteries, and waste collection; almost every service is run by the bureaucracy with only limited involvement by politicians. The choice between bureaucracy and democracy is a no-brainer, but America again walks alone on this one.

To the cynics and critics who point to the low voter turnout in America as evidence of a failing democracy, they do so from a standpoint of ignorance. Democracy is freedom of choice, and there is no greater freedom of choice than the democratic choice of not casting a vote. As discussed earlier, there is no perfect or true democracy, but nations that do offer voluntary voting as opposed to compulsory voting are closer to such a description. America does not pay mere lip service to the value of democracy as many other Western nations do; it epitomises it.

There are many other great differences between America and the Western World that are delivered by voluntary voting and the political system. Chief among these, apart from those already canvassed — such as freedom, primaries, and diversity of opinion — is a culture of giving, the elevation of democracy over bureaucracy, the increased role of think tanks, political activism, and absence of a 'talent drain' as is seen in other countries' governments.

While the American system does allow for a candidate with less than a majority of votes to prevail in elections where there are more than two candidates for a given office, it does not have the unfairness that can arise in a preferential system of voting where, unless voters fill out a monstrously large ballot in detail, their votes may flow to a candidate they do not support if the candidate they voted for is eliminated. This system allows party bureaucrats to assign to another party secondary or tertiary preferences that have not been specifically designated by the voter.

The American system has produced untold numbers of columnists, talk shows, and think tanks on both sides of the political equation that are essential disseminators of news and ideas and lead to a more acute and awakened democracy.

Alexis de Tocqueville in *Democracy in America* observed that the coming together of people in America to meet a common objective, made the country and its people unique. Unlike the UK, Australia, or even France, the name of whose legislative body, 'Parliament', refers to merely as a place of speech, the name of the United States' legislative assembly, 'Congress', actively refers to the process of having come together, *congressus* in Latin. Tocqueville noted that such acts of unity ensured that there was glue to the community and a broader outlook to the good of the nation. This, he said, led to an active political and civil society. This 'association' continues in America today, with political movements of all kinds existing.

One current example that springs to mind is the 'Tea Party' and its 'Freedom Rallies' in the conservative movement in America. Governments of either Republican or Democratic nature are never able to take the American people for granted, given their ability to organise and associate quickly and powerfully. Americans have what I venture to term a 'civic zeal'. Unlike the citizens of other nations, they are willing to make the time to take advantage of the political privileges bestowed upon them in order to ensure a better outcome for their community, not just for themselves—another symbol of the greatness of American culture. The words of famous ice hockey coach Herb Brooks to the US national team in the lead-up to what was ultimately America's greatest sporting moment—"Miracle on Ice"—sums up the American attitude toward politics and life: "When you pull on that jersey, you represent yourself and your teammates; and the name on the front is a hell of a lot more important than the one on the back!"

No chapter on American democracy and politics could be complete without an acknowledgement of state's rights, something that confuses non-Americans greatly. The residual sovereignty of states, as specifically designed by the framing of the Constitution, provides equilibrium with the federal government. Flexibility in democracy, an innate trait of any superior democracy, is not something Europeans do very well. For a continent that prides itself on diversity, and all the other wonderful applications of motherhood and tokenisms, the European Union allows far less difference in laws and regulation between its member nations than America does between its states. America has an exceptional democracy because the automatic impulse of Americans is to look locally, not centrally, for leadership and decisions.

Envy is also discernibly absent in American culture. As discussed in earlier chapters, envy is replaced by respect and admiration for successful people. Congruently, Americans consider their politicians, rightfully, as successful people, and rather than envy them, they instead aspire to emulate their success in life. Having toured six State Capitols, and the Capitol Building in Washington DC, I was struck by the opulence. From the Capitol Building's finely veined marble to its private subway system—a laudable efficiency for lawmakers—I could not help but think that only in America would there not be outrage at the luxury of a dedicated subway system for politicians.

In countries like Australia and Britain, the expenses of and use of resources by politicians are subject to tremendous media interest and public scrutiny, not to mention often vicious criticism of the existence of such perks. In Australia, the media will rarely go a month without revealing new figures on the Prime Minister's travel, or how much was spent on wine to entertain foreign dignitaries, or how much the replacement of chairs in the Parliamentary Lunch Room cost. It is this culture and attitude that leads me to believe that a luxury such as a private subway would provoke deafening criticism and opposition. The absence of envy in the American political milieu enables its people to respect public office holders and provides an incentive for others to strive for office.

This absence of envy also leads to another very clear difference between America and other Western democracies. In America, there is a respect for the office that a public official holds, quite apart from the person who holds the office. Americans may vehemently disagree with decisions made or harbour great reservations about performance, but they have a respect for the office that the person occupies.

Here I offer a personal story of an event I experienced as an elected representative in local government in Australia. One of our local McDonalds restaurants wished to extend their trade to a twenty-four hour operation. Their application was supported by local police and by the planning officers of the Council. The move was fiercely opposed by an organised group of residents who lived close-by on the basis of increased traffic, noise, and potential crime. When the matter came before the full Council meeting (comprising twelve elected representatives), some eighty residents showed up. After an hour and a half of listening to objections, it became clear that all the representatives except me, would side with the residents. When I rose and spoke in defence of McDonalds and pointed to their amazing charitable, environmental, and philanthropic work, the entire spectator gallery stood and turned their backs. It is difficult to imagine such disrespect for democracy in any public office in America.

Additionally, the focus of political activists in the American democratic system is ideology. Progressive and conservative ideology transcends the mainstream parties. Such activists form and organise to create an ideological grassroots movement. It is to these movements that 'renegade' elected representatives must answer, not to a centralised bureaucratic head office of a political party. As a result, unlike the ever-increasing convergence of the mainstream left and right parties in Australia and England, American politics is passionate, and politicians do not opt for the populist or 'soft' option. While many countries' political systems take the new path of 'least offence', America has shown immunity to it. The reason for this is again rooted in their values culture. Standing for something doesn't get in the way if you want to be in politics in America. It has not gone down the path of a race for the middle, or mediocrity, like many other Western democracies.

Interestingly, while Western nations such as Australia and Britain promote their credentials of freedom of speech and democracy, it is ironic that these are not actually practiced within the vehicles of democracy — major political parties. It may surprise Americans to learn that most major parties in Australia have set female quotas for candidates — that is to say, a certain number of candidates in any election must be women. Affirmative action in every area of life is the concept of those same people who see the rule of law as an impediment. This is what America avoids.

In Australian political parties, dissension, colour, or freedom of thought leads to marginalisation within the organization, or to expulsion. All of this can be summed up simply: In America, the best and brightest Americans are going into political office. (Some Americans may take umbrage at this, citing the emergence of the professional politician and declining standards, but this is a comparison.) In Australia and Britain, this is simply not the case. The strength of the political and democratic process in America results in great leadership, and this is another reason why America is one step ahead of other free societies.

IMPERILLED AMERICA

"Freedom is never more than one generation away from extinction. We didn't pass it on to our children in the bloodstream. It must be fought for, protected, and handed on for them to do the same, or one day we will spend our sunset years telling our children and our children's children what it was once like in the United States where men were free."

~Ronald Reagan, 40th President of the United States

MANY PEOPLE HAVE SUGGESTED that a book on American greatness is untimely because of the direction that the current administration is taking America and the unrest among Americans. Optimism must also deal with reality, and be topically relevant. For this reason, I have chosen to include this chapter.

This is a transcript of a speech I gave to a Freedom Rally on the steps of the Harrisburg, Pennsylvania Capitol on November 14, 2009:

Ladies and Gentlemen – My Friends of America,

The time has come to ring the bell of liberty.

I am Australian and you are American – and today we are united by the hallowed turf upon which we stand. We stand in the land that for so long has been a beacon of freedom, a moral oasis in the midst of a desiccated world desert.

It will take much to drain the liquid of freedom that has replenished this oasis over and over again, but it is fair to say the oasis faces its sternest and most unprecedented challenge yet.

I come to this podium today, knowing that your discontent travels the vast distance of your country. I come to this podium today knowing that a battle rages furiously under the clouds which have gathered over this magnificent land. I come to this podium today knowing that this battle is the topic of conversation all across America, wherever you go — from the booths tucked deep into the corners of suburban diners, to the hammocks that swing gently in the front porches of houses, to the cold elevators of secure apartment blocks, and in the car on the way to church on a Sunday morning. I know this because I have been there, and I've heard these conversations. The questions and concerns that all of you have about the country that you so dearly love are the same wherever you go: How do we save freedom and spread liberty? How do we protect American prestige? How do we defend American exceptionalism? How do we stop the country we love so much from becoming just another moribund European socialist state with unfettered government intervention and intrusion, limited entrepreneurial capacity for innovation, and flourishing political correctness?

But I come to this podium today, also, Ladies and Gentlemen, with a unique objective in all this: to inject some optimism into this battle. In doing so, I ask you not to rest your placards on the ground, turn heel, and march home, to lie supinely on your backs and hug to the delusive phantom that is hope. You have not done so and nor will you ever do so. To do so, would quite simply just not be the American way. Indeed, your reactions to the clouds that have gathered over your country, your presence here today and the rebirth of this very movement, remind me so much of the former words of British Prime Minister David Lloyd George.

Words that he offered as the First World War was poised to enter its fourth and ultimately final year, words that he offered about the Germans' expectations of the British coming into the war. He said: "It is not quite the story of the wolf and the lamb. I'll tell you why. Because they came expecting to find a lamb and instead they found a lion." And so the current administration finds you today.

For in that timeless American spirit, you have organised and mobilised in ways rarely before seen, in ways possible only here in this country – in the United States of America. Just as ... just as the founding fathers would recoil in horror at the actions of the current administration, they would rejoice in the knowledge that to the people that matter, their dreams are still so very much alive.

My friends, the time has come to ring the bell of liberty.

You are the people that matter. Limited government, low taxes, a strong national defence, a proud and unapologetic culture – these are the conditions, in history, under which we the people ... it is only under these conditions, that WE, the PEOPLE, have flourished and under which WE, the PEOPLE, seize opportunity and realise our dreams.

The time has come to ring the bell of liberty.

You are an exceptional people with an exceptional culture living in an exceptional country. I do not ask you to hug to false hope, but I do ask you in these dark hours to remember who you are and where you come from. That you are America and Americans. and that no stronger currency exists.

As you thumb through the pages of our history, you will be greeted with a record of American exceptionalism and endurance, with unprecedented economic, military, and entrepreneurial prowess – the envy of the world. And in this same book of history, you will find that it has always been in these times – when freedom has been under attack, when you have been numbed by adversity, when the tendency has been there to speak with a lump at the base of a parched throat — that the best of the American way has shone through. From the early defeats by Britain in the War of Independence, to the loss of the Philippines, to the days following Pearl Harbor, to that fateful day eight years ago in Washington, New York, and right here in this state, in Shanksville, Pennsylvania — when evil rocked the cradle of liberty — America emerged bigger, and stronger and better than ever before. And so it will again!

Ladies and Gentlemen, the time has come to ring the bell of liberty.

From the beaches of Normandy to the sands of Iraq, you have spread enormous democracy at an enormous cost, lest it be on the exalted soil of America that the most noble pursuit of mankind perish, in the land that has done so much for this noble idea.

Ladies and Gentlemen, saving freedom is our goal. Spreading liberty is our mission. We will not waver, stagger backward, nor be hemmed by foes. Tyranny is the poison that we must purge from our governments and our blood. Last year you were asked to chart a new course of hope and change. Today I stand before you and ask you to chart a different course, one much more familiar. Today, America, I beg you, for the good of your country, for the good of this world, to chart the old, well worn and well trodden course of freedom, to freedom for the people.

Despair not, for even if it is at the 59th second of the 59th minute of the eleventh hour, that bell of liberty will ring and victory will be ours. The home of the brave will once again be the land of the free. Thank you, Pennsylvania, God Bless You, and God Bless the United States of America!

Throughout this book, I have outlined my admiration of the United States and the need for it to stay true to the conservative principles of freedom, liberty, democracy, opportunity, justice, and bravery. I have shared with my audience my analysis of why America is the only values-driven country in the world today, and the role of patriotism, assimilation, religion, military and a culture of exceptionalism in achieving this. But this is all in danger.

American greatness is being imperilled by a number of statist and politically correct ambitions. These include an inclination to transform America to the type of paternalistic welfare state that we see in almost every other country in the Western World today. These inclinations are felt through various strains of increased government intervention, as evidenced by the bailouts and takeovers that the American government has participated in during the last two years. The feeling out among every day Americans is that freedoms are being lost, and there are no more checks and balances in the country so the government can and is getting away with it. The only way of restoring those checks and balances is by exercising a vote in the elections. People are sick of being taxed, and they worry about government debt. The fact is that America's current debt position is fundamentally unsustainable.

America is like nowhere else. Much of this, and all of its achievements as well as its culture, is a result of the relationship between government and citizen. Americans have always had a distrust of government, even in its earliest days. Americans are the most competitive and innovative because they are the sharpest. Where does this sharpness come from? It derives from the fact that, aside from private charity, there is no safety net. It is a survival-of-the-fittest mentality, the philosophy that delivers the greatest outcome in any social situation. If you remove these individualistic instincts from the American psyche, America becomes just a clone of the declining European socialist welfare state—and that is when American exceptionalism will cease to exist. That is what people in America so fear right now.

This is what the outside world does not understand. Americans, by nature—much like most of the English speaking world, due to cultural norms of the nuclear family—do not have the sense of entitlement and expectations of the state that Europeans have, for example. The increased and unprecedented activity of the state in people's lives in America means that the secret ingredient of American exceptionalism is nullified. I get it. Insecurity is the strongest form of motivation. America thrives on insecurity, and always has. It is not wrong or morally bankrupt to believe that man can achieve without the assistance of government; to the contrary, it is an admirable, profound belief in humanity.

The bloated welfare systems that appear right around the world have created a culture of dehumanised dependence and irresponsibility in those countries where they are in place, and those nations find themselves in an unenviable position. One need only look at Greece and its parlous state of affairs, with Spain and Portugal likely to join the distinguished club soon. This is why it is absurd to use modern Europe as a model for America in domestic and foreign policy, as the current American administration seem to contemplate. Europe is not a model for anything or anyone. From demography to policy to social cohesion, it is thoroughly finished. The nations of Europe have birth rates so far in decline—and sedation, inertia, and complacency have for so long been the default setting—it has very little to offer.

The other area of grave concern is the concept of cultural relativism and repeated public statements from the administration that it does not believe in American exceptionalism. This goes hand in hand with the intentions of bureaucratic internationalism abroad — to weaken nation-states and create a body that governs for many countries, not just one. For indications of just how dangerous the notion of cultural relativism can be, simply consider the politically correct edicts of radical multiculturalism and affirmative action in Western countries. These edicts have empowered minorities that are now the majority, and instead of gratitude, a new age of hostility has emerged from these very people. Their only form of assimilation is to be acutely aware of our weaknesses and capitalise on them. With the doctrine that every culture is equal in every country, is it any surprise that the new generations of previous immigrant generations are clueless about what their sense of identity should be?

Why should you believe in American exceptionalism? Aside from the fact that it is patently obvious, the answer is simple. Let us start with the fact that not all cultures are equal. This is a reality that many in the world find hard to accept. All human beings are equal, but not all cultures are equal. This may not sit comfortably with the "We Are The World" set, but it is reality. Every culture is flawed but some are certainly better than others. Cultural superiority can be established through objective facts, much the same way car sales or unemployment statistics may be used to measure the health of any advanced industrial democracy. These objective measures include the Human Development Index Ranking (awarded by the UN, of all places), GDP per capita, literacy, life expectancy, women's rights, and strength of democracy. A culture which oversees female genital mutilation, forced marriages, and honour killings, for example, is not the same as a culture which ensures equality before the law and provides freedom of speech. Any measurement of America using such objective instruments will show that America is indeed exceptional.

Another very important issue to discuss in this chapter is education. For education provides the key to the future, to success, to economic survival and to individual transformation. In America's case, it is the key to future generations and to continued American hegemony. Alexis de Tocqueville said about American education: "Americans are taught from birth that they must overcome life's woes and impediments on their own. Social authority makes them mistrustful and anxious, and they rely upon its power only when they cannot do without it. This first becomes apparent in the schools, where children play by their own rules and punish infractions [which] they define themselves." This is being directly challenged through government intervention and union collaboration. The sad reality is that the current American education curriculum has moved away from the curricula used up until the early 1990s. It has now become fashionable for education bureaucrats to look at historic exploration as genocide and American founding principles as suspect. By many measures, the US is lagging behind other countries in K-12 education.

American education must return to having the Pledge recited by classroom teachers in elementary school and by intercom in secondary schools. It must return to having flags in every classroom, gymnasium, lobby, and office. The Star Spangled Banner should be sung at athletic events and school assemblies. Constitution classes should be mandatory at secondary level. One year of elementary school should be devoted to US geography.

Importantly, history should be taught the way it actually happened, not with revisionist features and 'black armband' quality. American education must correct itself by being honest and proud about the American narrative. Washington's and Lincoln's birthdays should be celebrated in class with symbols of their honesty in particular: the cherry tree and returning change to a customer in New Salem. Columbus and other explorers should be presented as courageous innovators. Benjamin Franklin should be taught about as he really was — a universal man, universally revered. The Boston Massacre and the Boston Tea Party were great, courageous events. The Midnight Ride of Paul Revere poem and story should be included. The Revolution must be portrayed as the glorious event it was. John Adams and Thomas Jefferson should be focused on as Founding Fathers and important Presidents, followed later by Theodore Roosevelt, Woodrow Wilson and Franklin D. Roosevelt. Lewis and Clark were heroes. The great inventions should be taught — the steamboat, telegraph, steel plow, reaper, telephone, phonograph, assembly line — and all the men responsible for these inventions. The Civil War should be taught as the great moral triumph. Three Constitutional amendments, the 13th, 14th and 15th, accomplished end of slavery. The right of women to vote was a natural progression of liberalism. America's role in advancing democracy around the world should be mentioned. Tocqueville should be lauded in secondary textbooks, and studied in depth in senior years.

So there are some worrying concerns in America, but here's why I am and you should be optimistic. Firstly, Americans are currently exhibiting an uncommon valour, with their trademark disdain for docility. I just cannot imagine, given the strengths so apparent in America and its anti-socialist gut instincts, that its people will ever allow such a metamorphosis of culture and government. As opposed to the majority Western culture bred by reliance on government, the status quo is not sufficient for Americans if they are unhappy. They are, by and large, instinctively anti-authority with anti-government impulses and willing to take on government, more so than the populace of any other Western country, and that is to their great credit as well as advantage, in dealing with this threat.

Winston Churchill once wrote: "Socialism is the philosophy of failure, the creed of ignorance, and the gospel of envy." Failure, ignorance, and envy each represent the most vehement antithesis to the American life and culture. American culture may be described variously, but failure, ignorance, and envy are simply anathema to Americans and their lives. This is why America will never do socialism well.

Despite these ongoing threats, the United States is still the best country in the world today, as it has the most superior culture. Freedom, liberty and opportunity are at their most powerful in America. This is due to a synergistic combination of issues of culture such as morality and religion, patriotism, and the military. Those in the international world who suggest otherwise subscribe to the corrosive human elements of envy. The American spirit's philanthropic, passionate and community-oriented nature means Americans are able to mobilise in ways that support or impede actions. Since this is the case, while the American people must remain vigilant, they should also be eternally optimistic. More than any other nation or world superpower, America has displayed an uncanny propensity in history to recorrect itself. I have little doubt that this current angst and movement will be over soon, with strong evidence that the American trajectory is already being re-set.

Funnily enough, another twenty-six-year-old foreigner wrote long ago about this same phenomenon. Alexis de Tocqueville said, "The greatness of America lies not in being more enlightened than any other nation, but rather in her ability to repair her faults."

HOW GREATNESS ENDURES: THE FUTURE

*When the past no longer illuminates the future,
the spirit walks in darkness.*

~Alexis de Tocqueville, *Democracy in America*

MANY OUTSIDE AMERICA SUGGEST that the gradual decline of America has begun. Similarly, many suggest that the downfall of the United States is inevitable. Many who make these suggestions do so with glee, others with professional neutrality, few with disappointment. Their unity takes only one form. They are profoundly wrong.

The real American age has only just begun. The official reign of the United States began with the ending of the Second World War and continued with the victory of the Cold War and into this new century; but the true American age did not begin until September 11, 2001. This date marked the awakening of a sleeping giant by drawing cultural battlelines. This culture battle will see the United States not just victorious but also prospering. On that note, we also must recognise the outstanding leadership of the

English-speaking world by the Americans since the end of Second World War. What started in England with the Industrial Revolution in the early 1800s has continued to prosper in America into the new millennium.

Much of what will happen in the future is based on what has happened in the past. The history of America is long and proud, and it has exhibited courage and conviction on a scale never seen. The American narrative is truly unique. It is the most supreme superpower the world has ever witnessed. Through a fidelity to values that allow its people to thrive and innovate, America has made herself the greatest country in the world. Travelling through the United States, I sense a nation on the rise, not the wane. One gets the distinct feeling that America is in the relative infancy of greatness. There is an unshakeable feeling that something about American civilisation and strength is grandly unique. No other nation or people remotely competes with the values or natural strengths of America. It must not tolerate a decline in civic virtue.

The only challenge for America is to stay true to its values. It cannot fall victim to the same ills that felled the great European civilisations of the last two centuries, as discussed in the previous chapters. The anti-American agenda will seek to tempt America into doing so, as its agenda is fundamentally about undermining American confidence. The same agenda will form a marriage with political correctness to infest or dilute America's values. To this end, it is crucial that America maintain its trademark cockiness and arrogance. Without the protection of these traits, it becomes susceptible to the anti-American agenda. America must not be numbed by its maturity as a nation or succumb to the more elderly characteristics of impotence and risk aversion. It must stay true to itself.

American greatness will maintain its superiority through two primary sources: human capital and structural capitalism. In terms of human capital, the ingenuity, commitment and work ethic of the American people simply have no peer. The twin values of striving for excellence and dreaming allows America to think big and be at the forefront of every industry. It has a disdain for government and the pursuit of mediocrity. American educational institutions are not just world-class; they lead the world. The financial endowments provided to such institutions mean that they have a far greater focus on research and development. The leaders of the United States are more often than not graduates of these institutions, which mean that US leadership will always have the edge on other countries' leadership quality. It is no accident that the language of computers is English. Strategically, it is very important that all code is in English as technology is so crucial to running the world.

The structure of American capitalism lends itself more than does any other brand of capitalism as an incentive for work and innovation. Level of benefit is commensurate with amount of work. A small example is the American capital gains tax of roughly fifteen percent, compared with Australian capital gains tax of roughly thirty percent. The investment inclination of the capitalist structure fits well with the risk-taking culture and suggests a much deeper belief and faith in people than does any other culture. The economies in America are economies of scale, due to large populations. While a federal government unites the nation, there is a paradoxical state-centric focus to government and democracy in America. This breeds competition between the states, which leads to a better outcome for all. For example, if one state decides to offer tax concessions within a certain industry, then another state must match such concessions or lose industry and populace to another state. More than any of this, though, is the strength and flexibility provided by America's political system and the way this causes Americans to look to local rather than to centralised authority for solutions.

Unlike many countries around the world, the United States will continue to increase in population. Many suggest that this is problematic in that it will result from immigration as opposed to American births. Those who do so ignore the unique ability America has shown throughout its history to fundamentally integrate great swathes of their incoming immigrant population into their culture, institutions and existing national identity. The demographics issue is an enormous one and is another reason for my prediction of continued American success. The only nations, other than America, in the Western world that are relatively close to population replacement rate are Australia, New Zealand, and Ireland.

The fact is that the policies of American governments until this moment have encouraged and fostered an environment for the traditional family and, as a result, America's birth rate is still virtually at replacement rate. This is yet another reason why America can ill afford to pursue the path of entitlement and expectation of largesse from government.

The United States has several natural advantages: its geographic position, natural resources, and population size. In terms of natural resources, there is an abundance of coal, natural gas, and other sources of energy. The massive population means an abundance of workers. It was also blessed to have remarkable Founding Fathers. These men were scholars who first conducted extensive research on earlier republics and proceeded to devise a sense of government and society unlike any the world has ever seen.

This achievement has allowed people around the world to consider America as not just a country but as an identity. This identity has almost intangible qualities, but one quality is discernibly tangible: America equals freedom. One of the greatest pointers toward America continuing its leadership role in the free world is a robust, emerging trend that receives little media attention or academic analysis. The developing world loves America and wants to be like America. These people desire freedom of religion. They want the oppressed to be freed. Lithuania, Poland, Eastern Europe, Africa, parts of Latin America, and a growing silent minority across the Middle East feel the same way.

It is my belief that no other country can come close to usurping America. In my view, the only way that this is possible is for another country to simply copy America. But here is the problem: Every other country is in stasis. Economic and cultural differences coupled with most countries' anti-American tendencies means that no other nation will ever be willing to copy America.

The future of American hegemony is often viewed in the context of the emergence of China, much the same way that the USSR was once viewed — that is, another country becoming the new superpower. Looking at the world today, I do not see any other nation that is remotely within striking range of superpower status. China is inherently unstable internally, with limited resources and a problematic gender imbalance in their population, just to begin with. India has potential, but the presence of corruption, social and religious strains, and the fact that it is not a developed country and has millions in poverty and starvation, means that its rise is a long way off. Russia may be the largest country in the world and hostile, but it also has demographic and health problems; frankly, it does not even rate in a discussion. No other country can come close to usurping America unless it replicates it, and pride makes them unwilling to copy the American model.

The reality is that this frame of analysis in evaluating likely successors of America as superpowers is not relevant in today's world. More likely is a world where no country is a superpower, which would suit the ambitions of many forces in the world and is supported by UN types. The bad news is that this has become the general trend of the world. The good news is that the outcome of this rests entirely in the hands of America. It is only if they, through the government they elect, acquiesce to the desires of the secular intellectual class, deny American exceptionalism, and adopt the edicts of relativism that this will happen.

Radical Islamism is also a threat to American power. The demographics of Europe, aided through welfare programs in those nations and their politically correct policies, means that Islamic power in the world is increasing. The only comfort on that front is that if you look at the Middle East and study the modern Muslim nations, it is unambiguously evident that their only strengths are making babies and hating the West. They are unproductive, regressive, and stagnant in terms of innovation. America must exercise caution and not embrace the domestic policies of its Western cousins on immigration and multiculturalism, for these hold great danger for potential home- grown terrorism and disharmony. Current proposals like the one before New York City for an Islamic Centre on or near Ground Zero must be soundly and overwhelmingly rejected. The idea is as offensive as it is absurd. America must not allow its tolerance to be so brazenly taken advantage of, as have many other countries.

The common thread of anti-Americanism is to concentrate on America in basic terms: "guns, crime, poverty, no-go zones, a society of haves and have-nots, of great luxury alongside great poverty" is the refrain. Resentment, envy, and misunderstanding characterise the outside world's view of America. Why change? Why react? America does not and should not seek to appease or conform to an agenda driven by, at best, misjudgement, and at worst, revulsion based on covetousness.

Ignoring for a moment even the selectiveness and inaccuracy of this agenda, many miss the point. America is bigger than a country; it is an idea. While America and its demographics, culture, and governments may have changed and will continue to change, America as a concept, as an idea, endures. America is strong, free, and independent, fashioned on the visions of its Founding Fathers. It isn't perfect, but American culture is about loving winners, seizing opportunity, and fulfilling dreams. The culture is transcendental, while simultaneously buoyant, bold and rewarding. America is an exceptional country because of an exceptional culture that breeds exceptional people. It must keep its culture intact. It simply cannot afford to change.

I believe that many Americans do not realise how great they are or their impact on the world; nor do they understand how much America, the entity, can do for the world. While American leadership must continue to be uncompromising, using whatever military or economic means are available to achieve its outcomes, first and foremost, a secondary consideration is that it must not forget the power it wields in spreading American innovation and medical advances across the world.

Much has been made in this book about America's inherent goodness, through its values and by examination of charity, philanthropy, military intervention, and the spread of freedom through disseminating American identity and culture. The quick way, however unlikely it is, that America could lose its way in the future would come if it ever departs from this. Alexis de Tocqueville's most famous words are more poignant than ever: *"America is great because America is good. If America ceases to be good, America will cease to be great."*

Another simple but easily forgotten point: for America to continue to lead the world in freedom and hope, those conditions must continue to define the American existence at home.

I want to leave you with the most emotionally powerful experience of my trip. One of the legs of my speaking tour was spent in New York City. After delivering my speech at the Soldiers', Sailors', Marines', Coast Guard & Airmen's Club, a young African-American lady sought me out. It turned out she was a volunteer for the Wounded Warrior Project, an organisation dedicated to providing services and programmes for severely injured service men and women. She said, "Your message must be heard by the New York firefighters. I work with them and they will love you. You must come with me tomorrow, and I will take you around to as many firehouses as we can fit in." She knew the firefighters of various firehouses around the city because, in her volunteer work, she would organise the firefighters to sign and provide well wishes on cards to send both to current Wounded Warriors, many in Walter Reed Hospital, and to those still serving in Afghanistan and Iraq. I was given a personal tour of many fire stations all across New York, during which I met and spoke with dozens of New York's bravest, and spread my message. The fire stations are all patriotic and nostalgic venues, resplendent with American flags, and one really feels the heroism of the New York firefighter.

The firehouse that had the greatest impact was the FDNY Ten House, Ladder 10, Engine 10, located in Liberty

Street, directly across the road from where the World Trade Center once stood. It is the best known firehouse in the world. I had the enormous honour of meeting firefighter and hero John Morabito, a driver for Ladder 10, whose story of incredible survival has been the subject of much media attention. As I heard his harrowing account of that day from morning to end while he showed me around the firehouse, from the sound of those trapped who chose to jump, to being unable to drive due to the dead bodies lying on Liberty Street, to the loss of his six colleagues, to the complete annihilation of the firehouse, I felt sick. How could a city, a people, a nation ever recover from this? But they have. As President Bush said: "Here buildings fell, and here a nation rose."

The story of Ladder 10 and John Morabito and the way this firehouse responded, not just on that day, but in the years immediately after, is not only awe-inspiring and heart-warming, it exemplifies exactly why America is the incredible nation that it is today. The fifty-six-foot FDNY Memorial Wall on the side of the firehouse, as well as the 'Ten House Bravest 9-11 Memorial' inside, are testament to America's ability to remember and appreciate. John Morabito told me that since that fateful day, people have asked him why he never sought professional therapy. His answer to the question he is always asked? "Nick, this is my therapy. Sitting on the front of this firetruck and talking to people every day, telling my story." Going into the future, America can be comforted that there are millions of John Morabitos. They can also rest well knowing that today's New York firefighter spirit represents what every American has bubbling inside them: exceptional patriotism, a belief in Providence, a love of the military, a devotion to freedom, and a disposition to bravery.

'Amerocracy' should be the mindset of people all around the world who love freedom, democracy, liberty, and justice. To be an 'Amerocrat' is to support the country that is truly the land of the free and the home of the brave, regardless of where you live. It is fitting that a formal ideology represent the views of the silent majority comprising hundreds of millions around the world who are deeply inspired by the United States and feel their countries would do well to learn from the United States.

In our own way, all free people are Americans.

Stay the course, America.

ACKNOWLEDGEMENTS

Three books were absolutely pivotal to helping me develop my ideas and arguments in this book. They are Alexis de Tocqueville's *Democracy in America*, Mark Steyn's *America Alone: The End of the World As We Know It*, and Bronwen Maddox's *In Defence of America*.

Many people made this book happen.

I want to thank my American friends. I single out John Parrott and Mickey Straub for special mention.

To the former Prime Minister of Australia and the greatest one my country has ever had, John Howard: I extend an enormous thank you for educating a generation of people my age of American greatness, and the importance of the standing by our American cousins, and having the courage to protect our Western culture.

LaVergne, TN USA
28 November 2010

206508LV00006B/64/P